Transformers Energon™ Brand

A New Threat

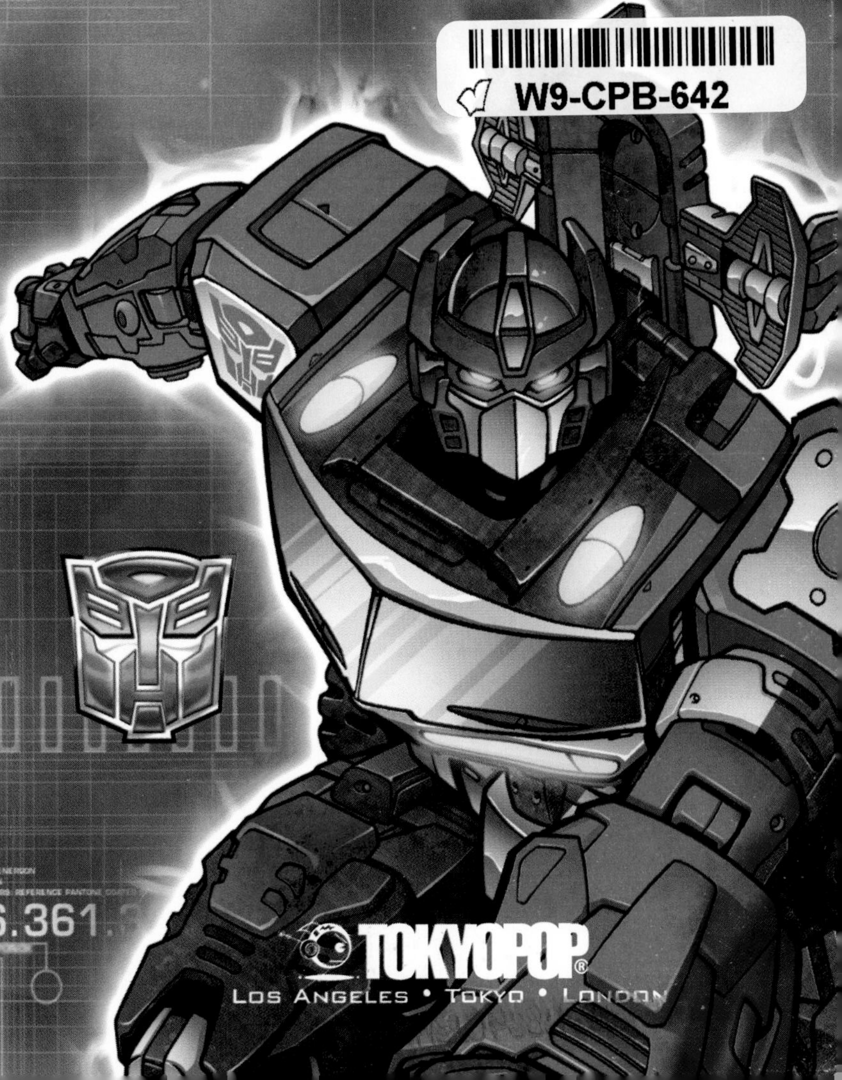

TOKYOPOP®
Los Angeles • Tokyo • London

Contributing Editor - Tim Beedle & Amy Court Kaemon
Graphic Design & Lettering - Atomic PDX
Graphic Artists - Jennifer Nunn-Iwai & Tomás Montalvo-Lagos
Cover Layout - Harlin Harris

Editors - Elizabeth Hurchalla & Jod Kaftan
Digital Imaging Manager - Chris Buford
Pre-Press Manager - Antonio DePietro
Production Managers - Jennifer Miller, Mutsumi Miyazaki
Art Director - Matt Alford
Managing Editor - Jill Freshney
VP of Production - Ron Klamert
President & C.O.O. - John Parker
Publisher & C.E.O. - Stuart Levy

Come visit us online at www.TOKYOPOP.com

A TOKYOPOP® Cine-Manga™
TOKYOPOP Inc.
5900 Wilshire Blvd., Suite 2000, Los Angeles, CA 90036

Published and distributed by TOKYOPOP Inc., Los Angeles, CA, U.S.A.

ISBN: 1-59182-817-1

First TOKYOPOP® printing: May 2004

10 9 8 7 6 5 4 3 2 1

Printed in Canada

TRANSFORMERS ENERGON ™ BRAND

CONTENTS

CHARACTER BIOS

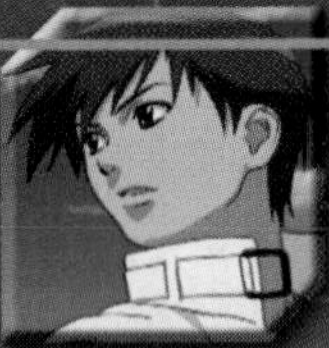

KICKER

A rebellious kid who lives on Earth.

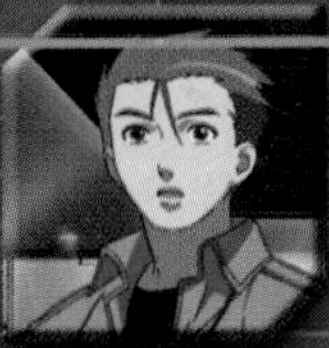

RAD

One of the Autobots' best allies.

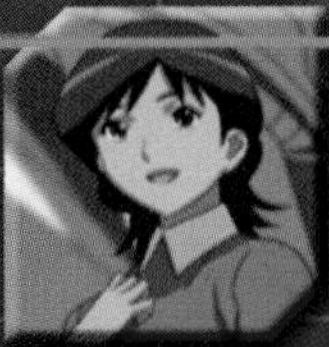

ALEXIS

A VIP who works for the Earth Federation.

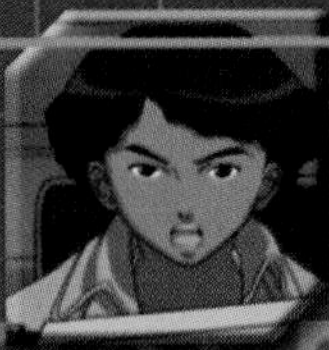

CARLOS

Rad's best friend.

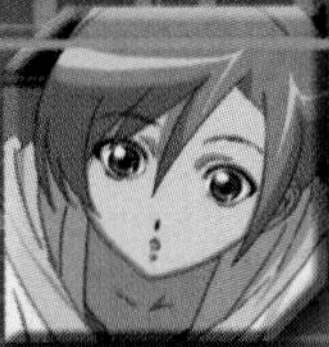

SALLY

Kicker's younger sister.

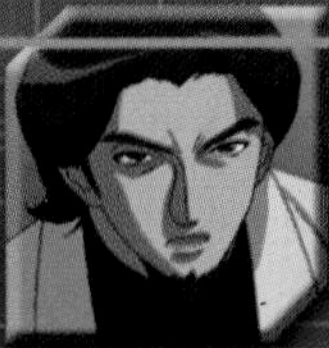

DR. JONES

A scientist who is Kicker and Sally's father.

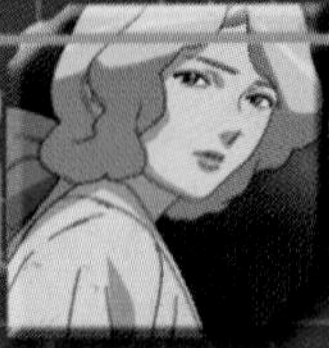

MIRANDA

Kicker and Sally's mother and also a scientist.

OPTIMUS PRIME

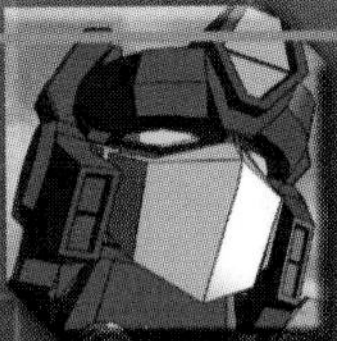

The leader of the Autobots, he transforms into an 18-wheeler truck.

HOT SHOT

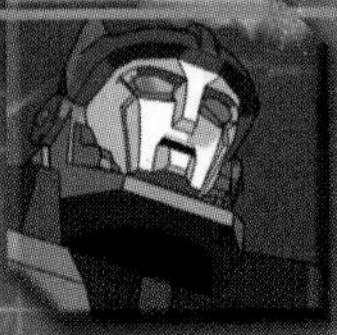

A young and heroic Autobot who transforms into a sports car.

JETFIRE

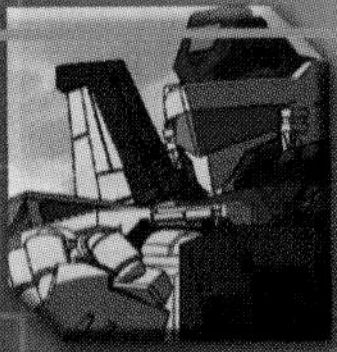

A swift and stealthy Autobot who transforms into a powerful space shuttle.

IRONHIDE

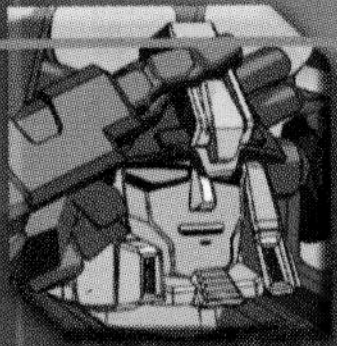

An energetic and eager young Autobot who transforms into a 4x4 with a powerful cannon.

INFERNO

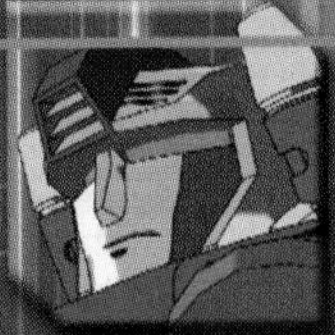

A skilled and brave Autobot who transforms into a fire truck.

ALPHA Q

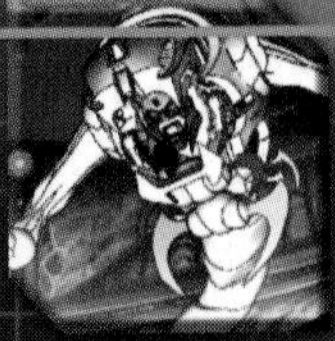

The evil power core of Unicron.

THE TERRORCONS

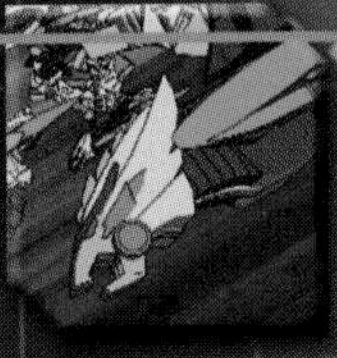

A group of predatory Transformers.

TransFormers
ENERGON ™ BRAND

CYBERTRON CITY

ENGLISH ADAPTATION: TERRY KLASSEN

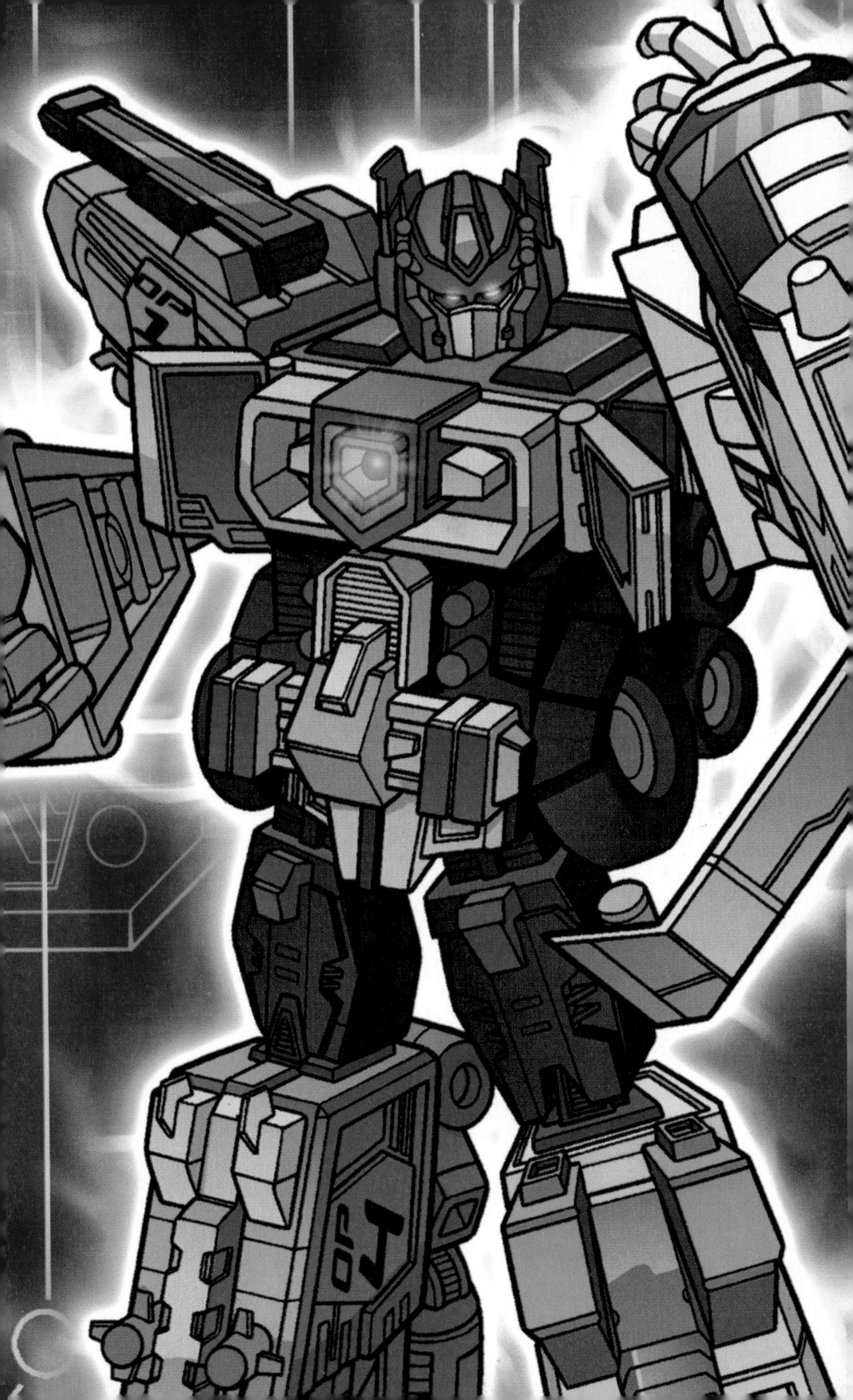

Prologue...

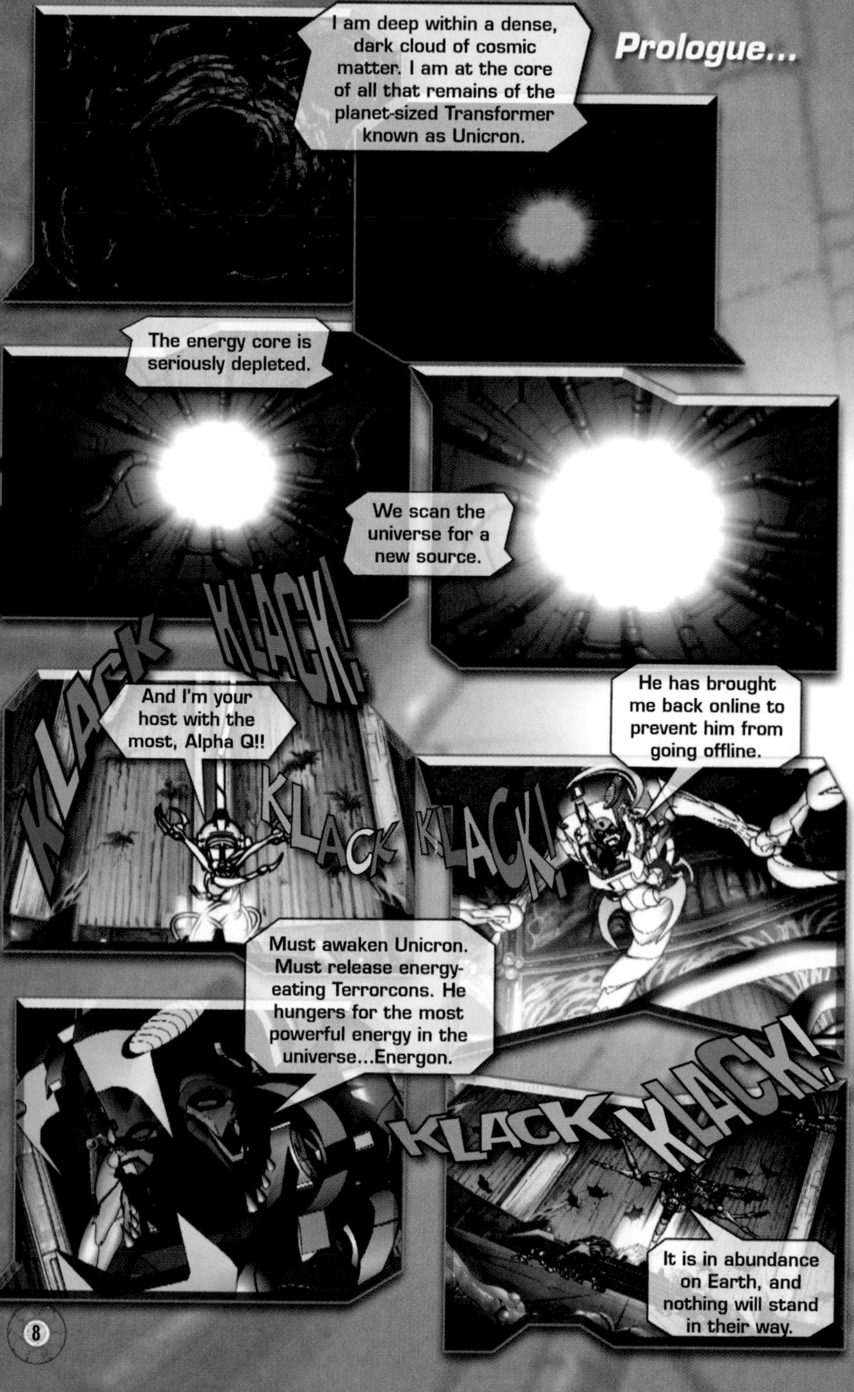

I am deep within a dense, dark cloud of cosmic matter. I am at the core of all that remains of the planet-sized Transformer known as Unicron.
The energy core is seriously depleted.
We scan the universe for a new source.
KLACK KLACK!
And I'm your host with the most, Alpha Q!!
KLACK KLACK!
He has brought me back online to prevent him from going offline.
Must awaken Unicron. Must release energy-eating Terrorcons. He hungers for the most powerful energy in the universe...Energon.
KLACK KLACK!
It is in abundance on Earth, and nothing will stand in their way.

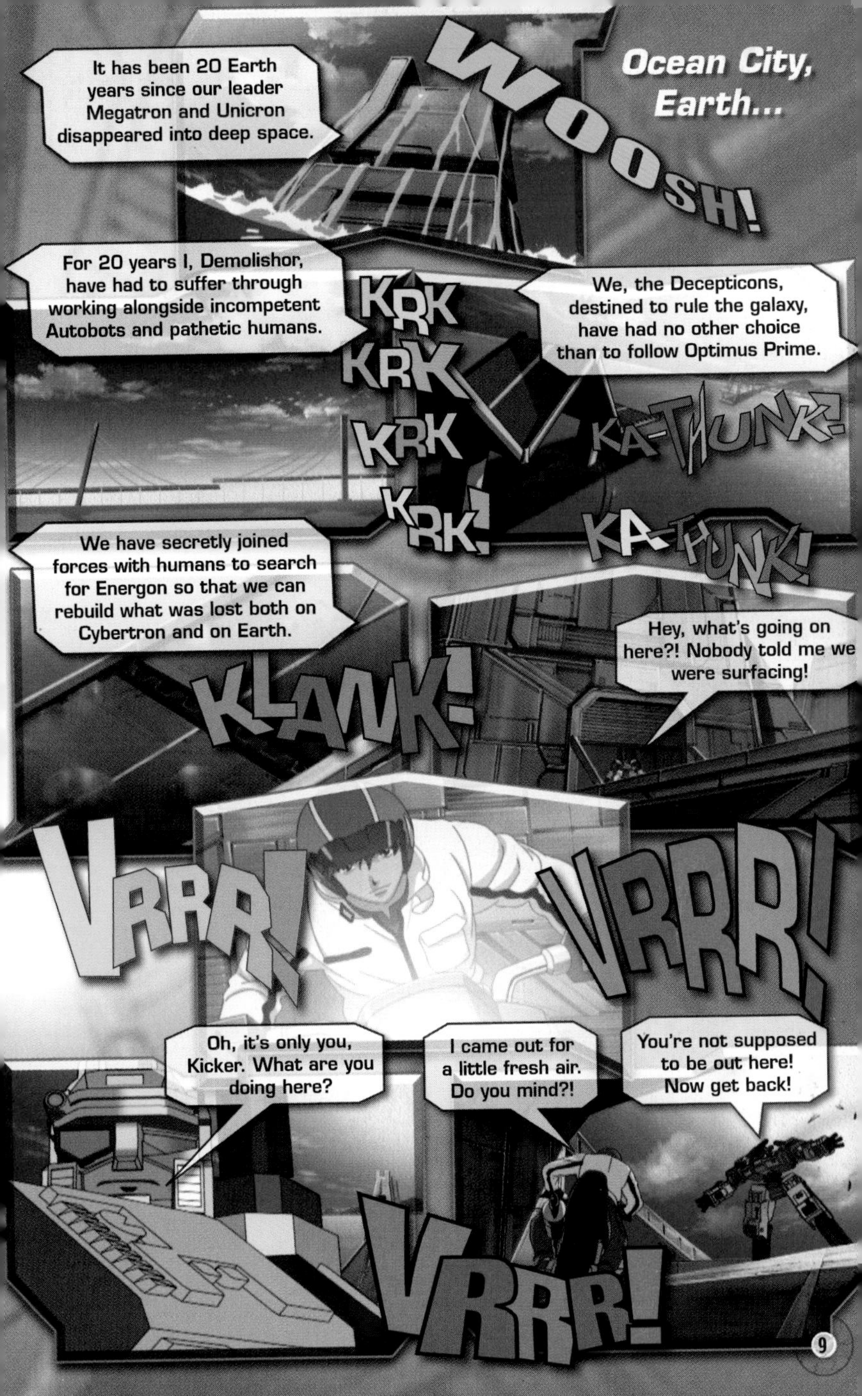

It has been 20 Earth years since our leader Megatron and Unicron disappeared into deep space.
Ocean City, Earth...
WOOOSH!
For 20 years I, Demolishor, have had to suffer through working alongside incompetent Autobots and pathetic humans.
KRK KRK KRK KRK!
We, the Decepticons, destined to rule the galaxy, have had no other choice than to follow Optimus Prime.
KA-THUNK!
KA-THUNK!
We have secretly joined forces with humans to search for Energon so that we can rebuild what was lost both on Cybertron and on Earth.
KLANK!
Hey, what's going on here?! Nobody told me we were surfacing!
VRRR!
VRRRR!
Oh, it's only you, Kicker. What are you doing here?
I came out for a little fresh air. Do you mind?!
You're not supposed to be out here! Now get back!
VRRR!

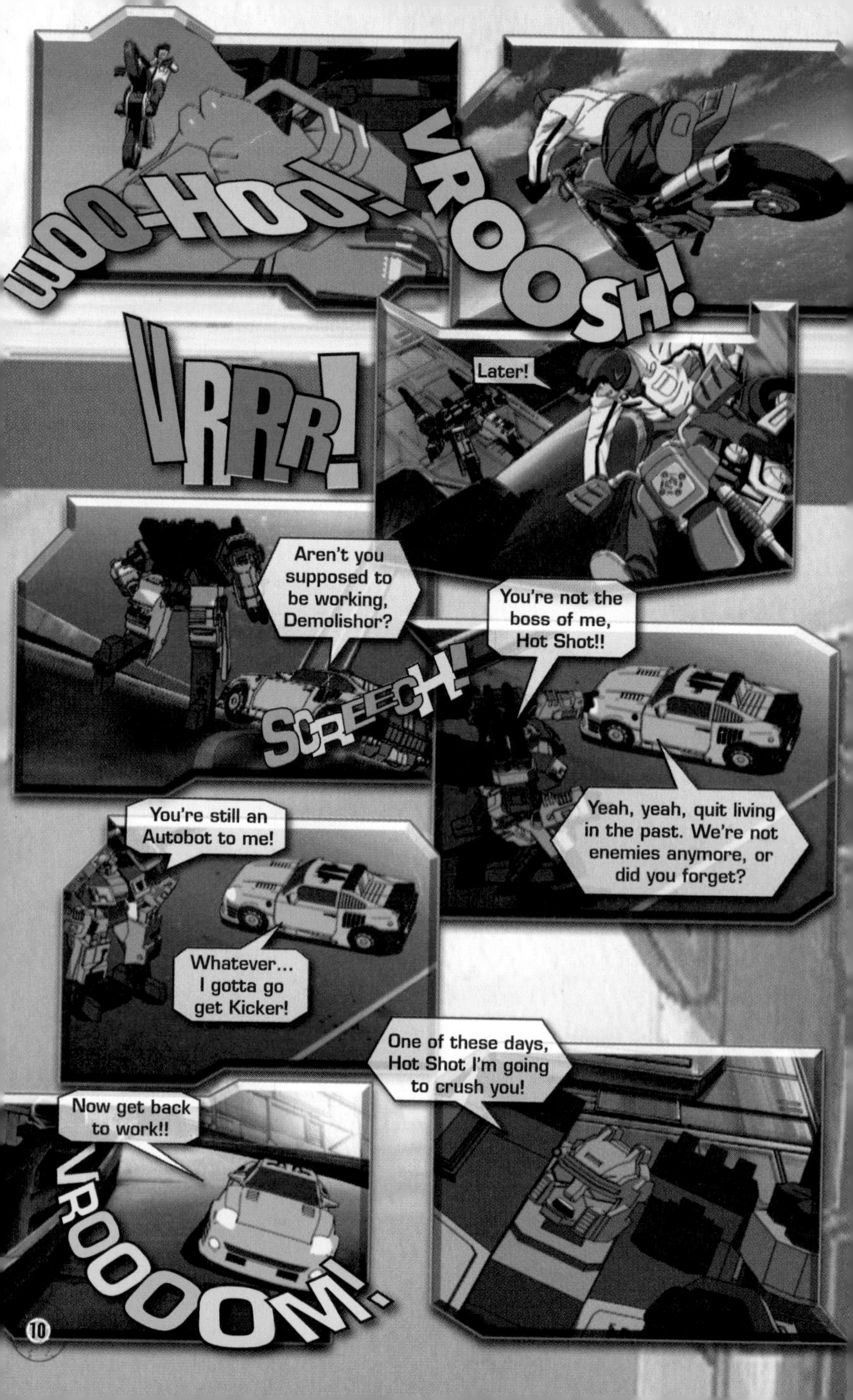

WOO-HOO!
VROOSH!
VRRR!
Later!
Aren't you supposed to be working, Demolishor?
SCREECH!
You're not the boss of me, Hot Shot!!
Yeah, yeah, quit living in the past. We're not enemies anymore, or did you forget?
You're still an Autobot to me!
Whatever... I gotta go get Kicker!
Now get back to work!!
VROOOOM!
One of these days, Hot Shot I'm going to crush you!

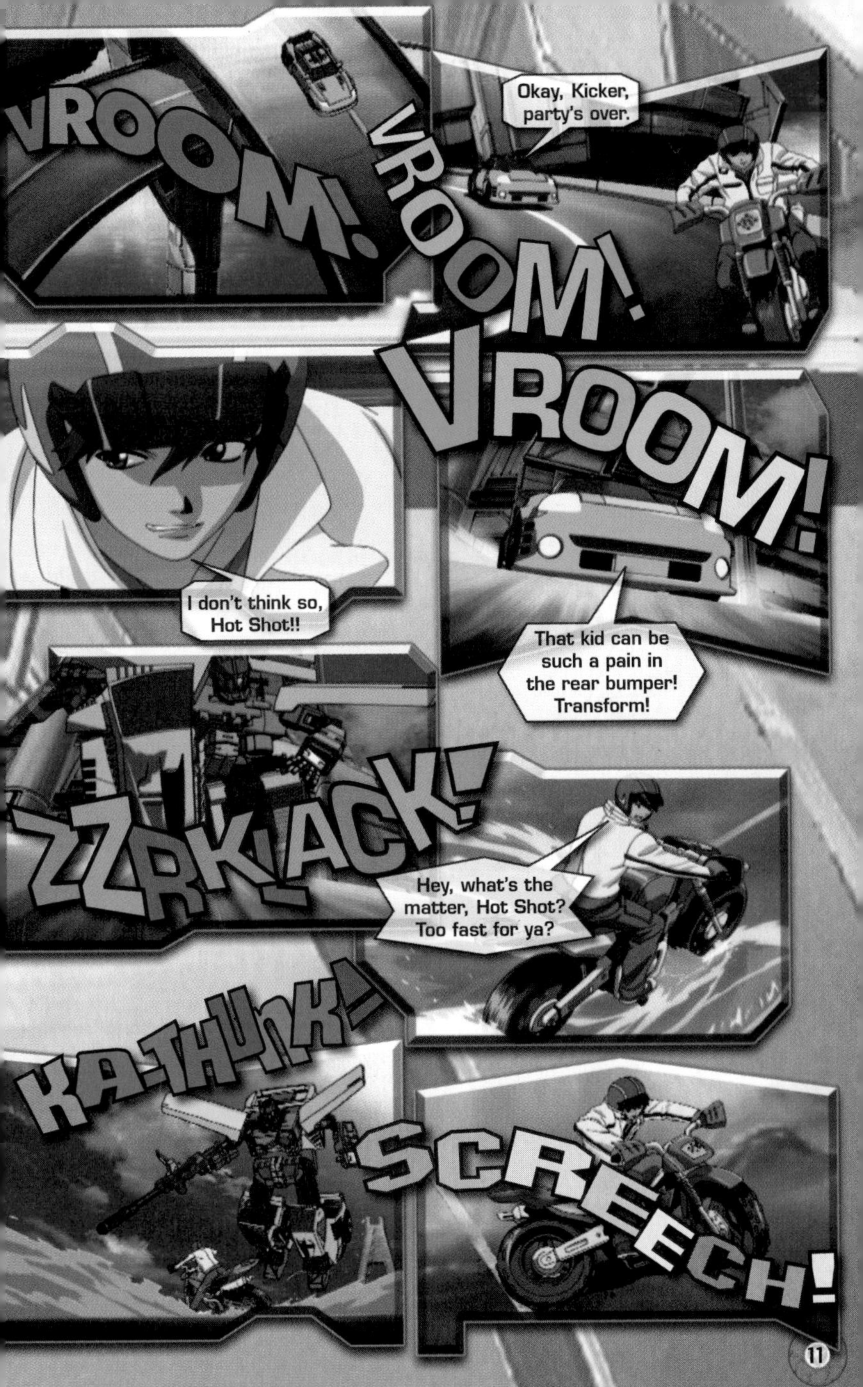
VROOM!
Okay, Kicker, party's over.
VROOM!
VROOM!
I don't think so, Hot Shot!!
That kid can be such a pain in the rear bumper! Transform!
ZZRKLACK!
Hey, what's the matter, Hot Shot? Too fast for ya?
KA-THUNK!
SCREECH!

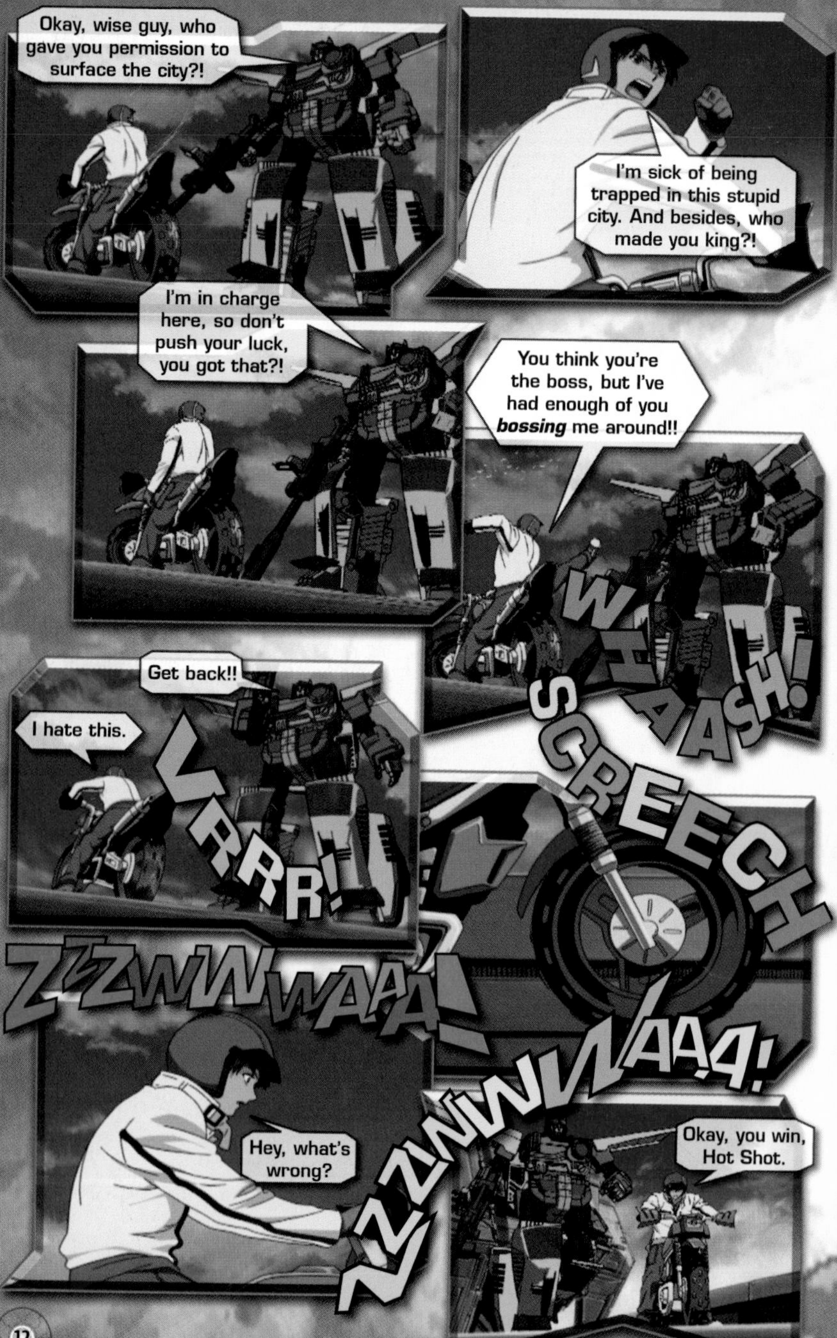
Okay, wise guy, who gave you permission to surface the city?!
I'm sick of being trapped in this stupid city. And besides, who made you king?!
I'm in charge here, so don't push your luck, you got that?!
You think you're the boss, but I've had enough of you ***bossing*** me around!!
WHAASH!
Get back!!
I hate this.
VRRRR!
SCREECH
ZZZWWWAAA!
Hey, what's wrong?
ZZZWWWAAA!
Okay, you win, Hot Shot.

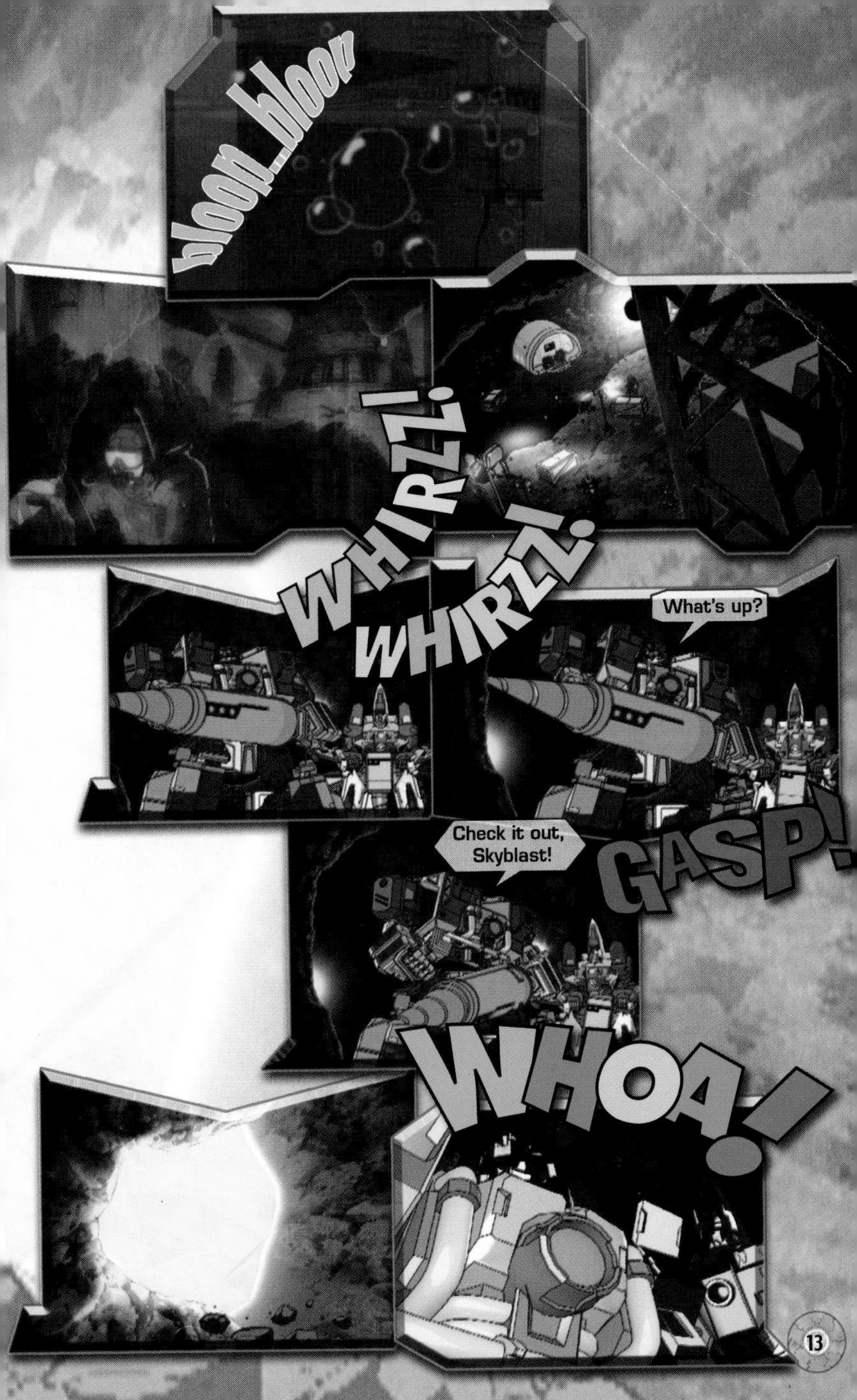
bloop...bloop
WHIRZZ!
WHIRZZ!
What's up?
Check it out, Skyblast!
GASP!
WHOA!

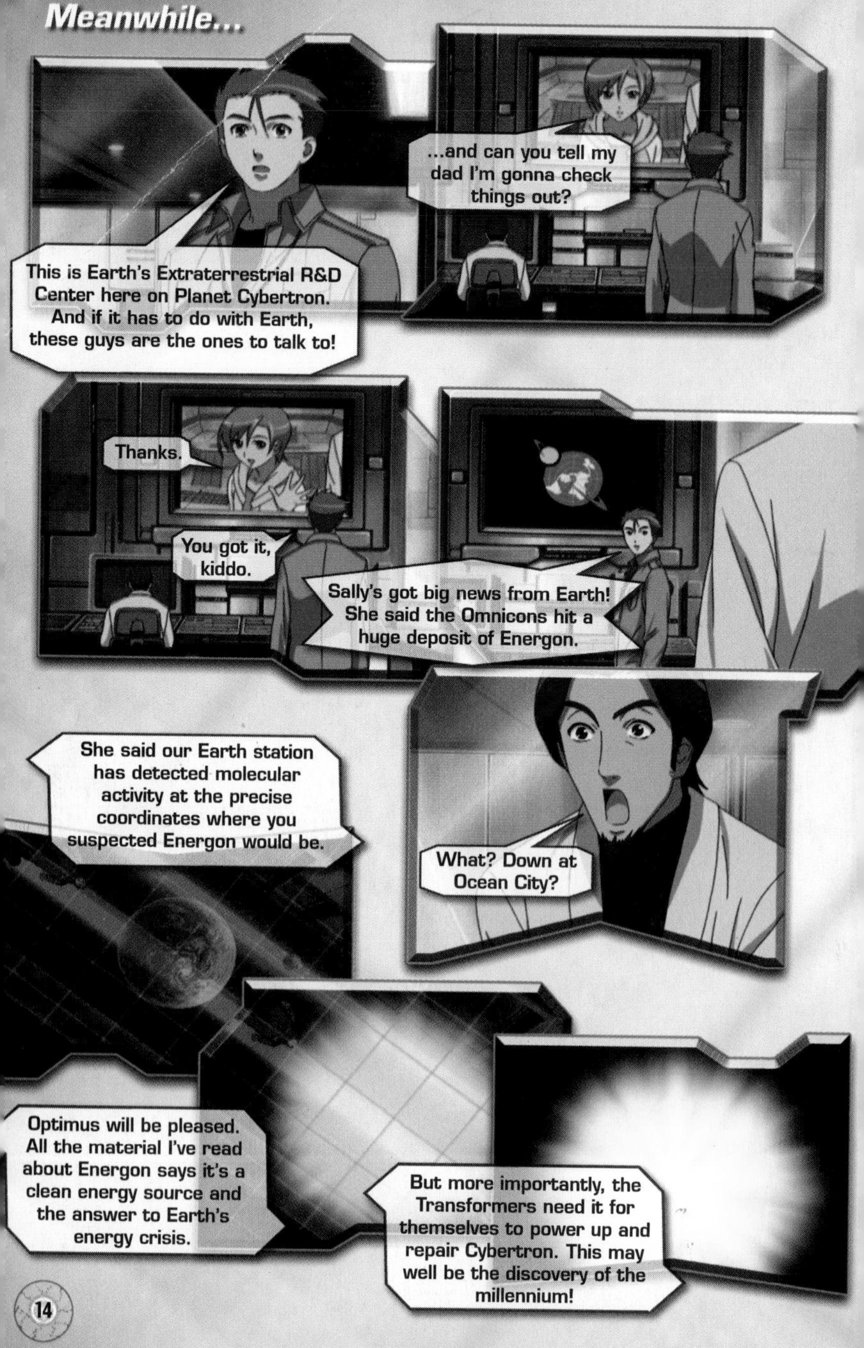

Meanwhile...
This is Earth's Extraterrestrial R&D Center here on Planet Cybertron. And if it has to do with Earth, these guys are the ones to talk to!
...and can you tell my dad I'm gonna check things out?
Thanks.
You got it, kiddo.
Sally's got big news from Earth! She said the Omnicons hit a huge deposit of Energon.
She said our Earth station has detected molecular activity at the precise coordinates where you suspected Energon would be.
What? Down at Ocean City?
Optimus will be pleased. All the material I've read about Energon says it's a clean energy source and the answer to Earth's energy crisis.
But more importantly, the Transformers need it for themselves to power up and repair Cybertron. This may well be the discovery of the millennium!

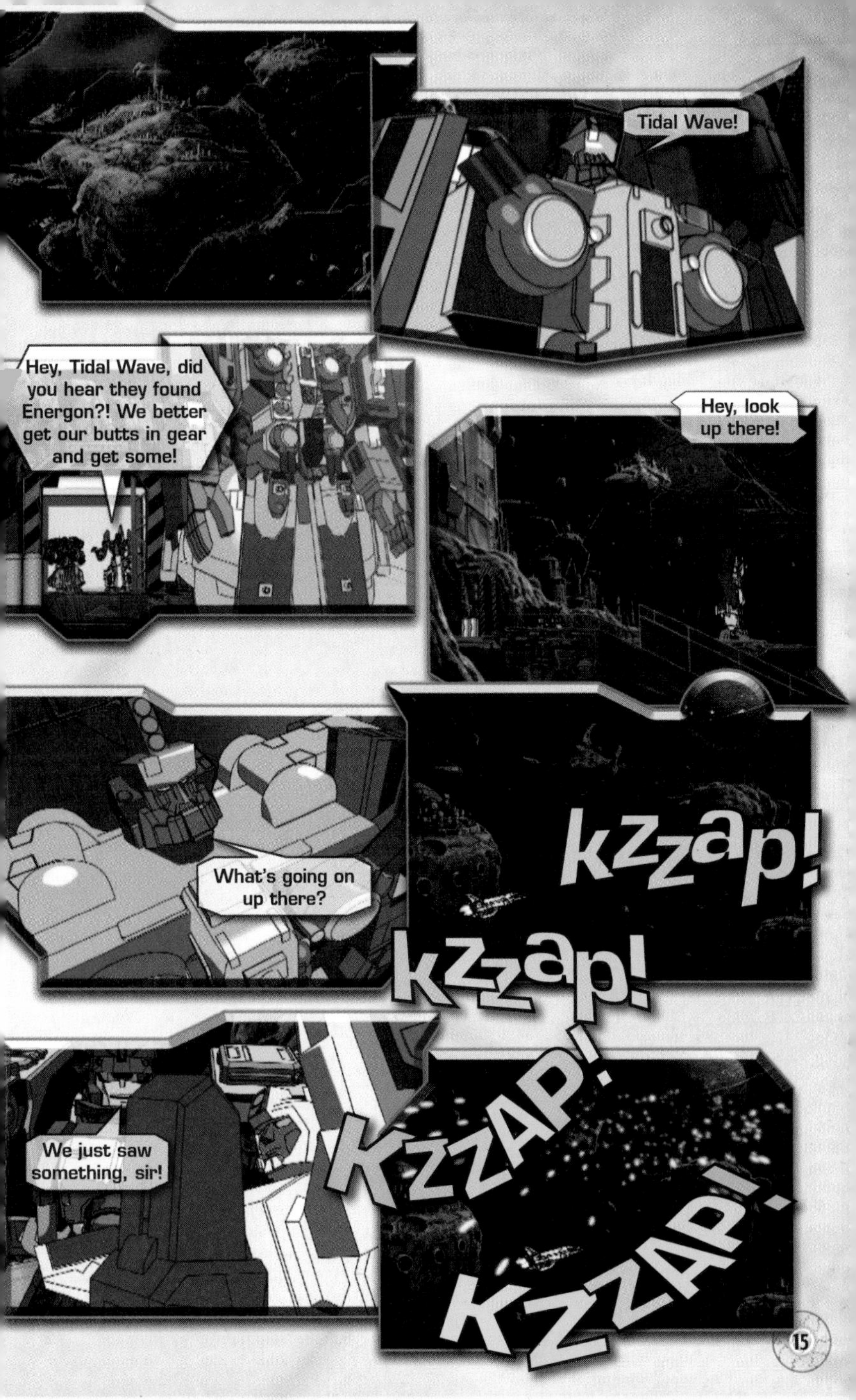
Tidal Wave!
Hey, Tidal Wave, did you hear they found Energon?! We better get our butts in gear and get some!
Hey, look up there!
What's going on up there?
kzzap!
kzzap!
We just saw something, sir!
KZZAP!
KZZAP!

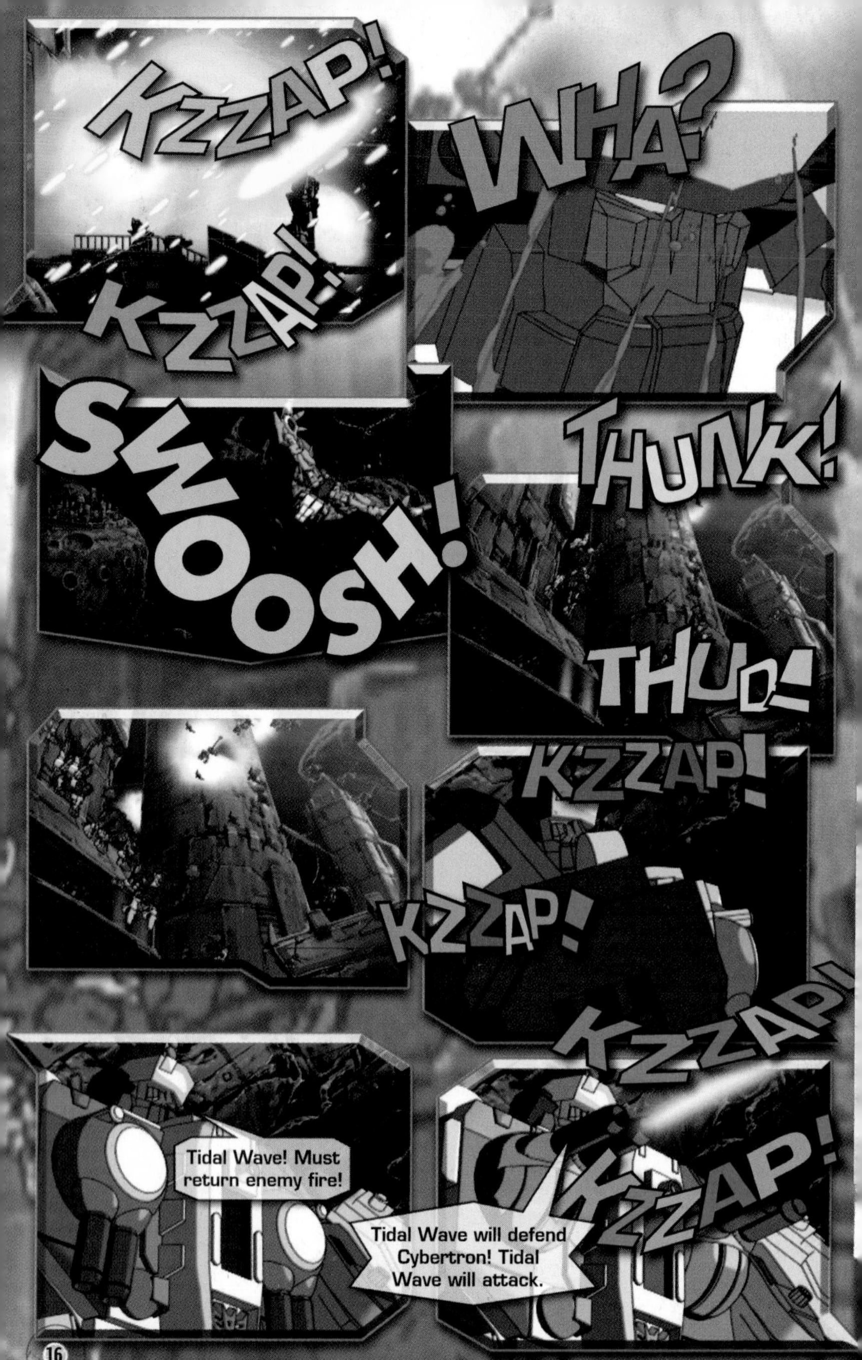
KZZAP!
KZZAP!
WHA?
SWOOSH!
THUNK!
THUD!
KZZAP!
KZZAP!
Tidal Wave! Must return enemy fire!
Tidal Wave will defend Cybertron! Tidal Wave will attack.
KZZAP!
KZZAP!

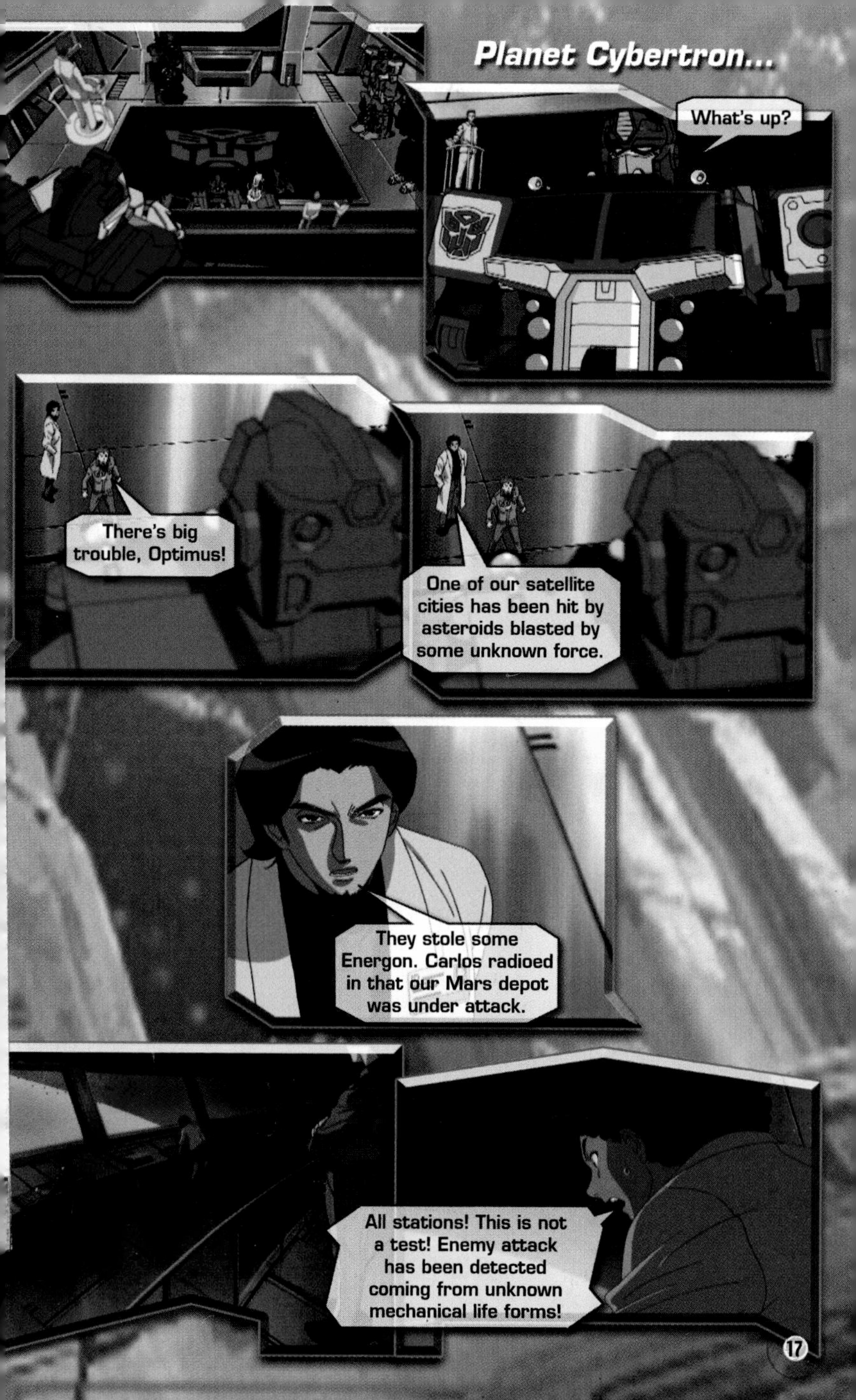
Planet Cybertron...
What's up?
There's big trouble, Optimus!
One of our satellite cities has been hit by asteroids blasted by some unknown force.
They stole some Energon. Carlos radioed in that our Mars depot was under attack.
All stations! This is not a test! Enemy attack has been detected coming from unknown mechanical life forms!

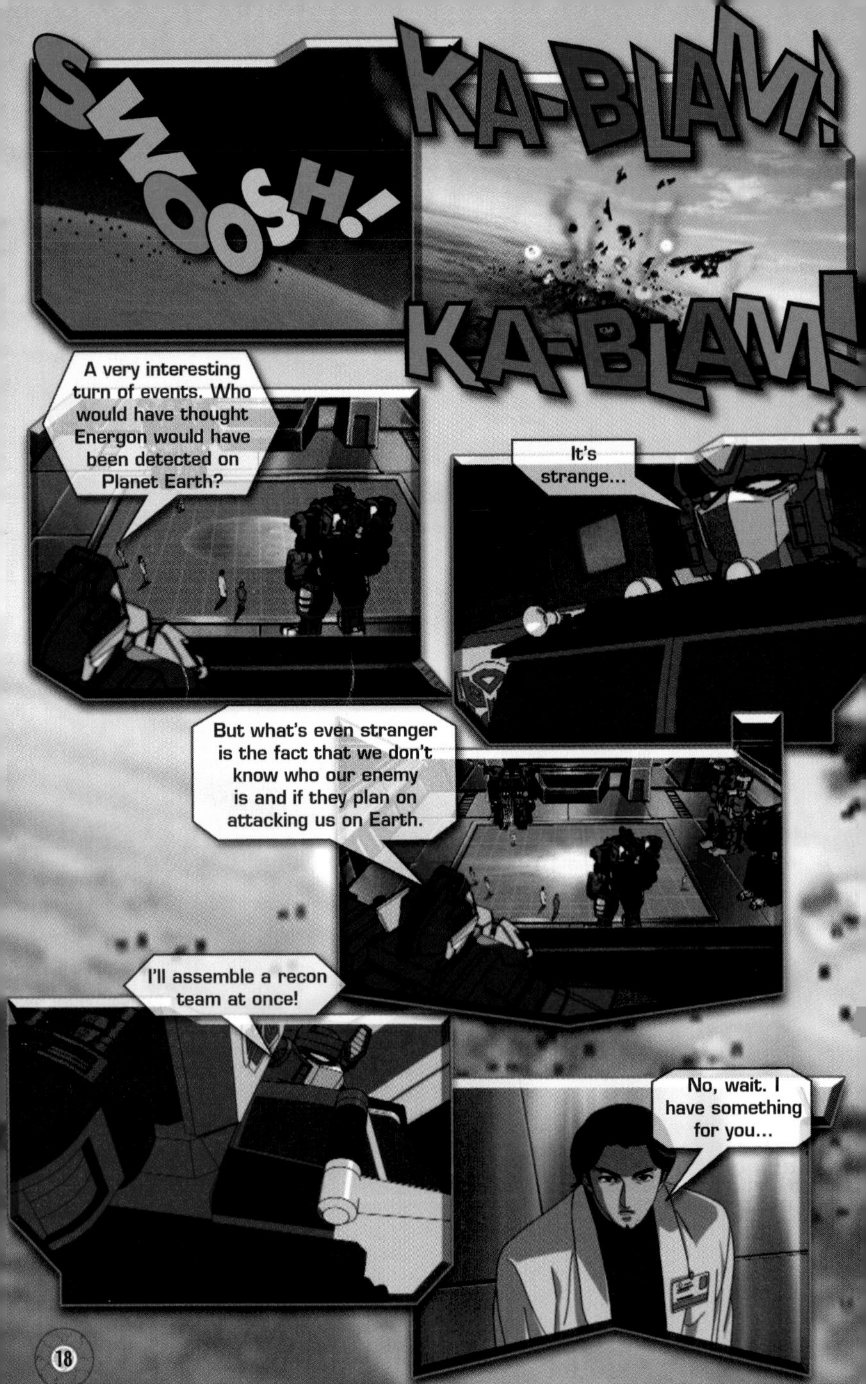
SWOOSH!
KA-BLAM!
KA-BLAM!
A very interesting turn of events. Who would have thought Energon would have been detected on Planet Earth?
It's strange...
But what's even stranger is the fact that we don't know who our enemy is and if they plan on attacking us on Earth.
I'll assemble a recon team at once!
No, wait. I have something for you...

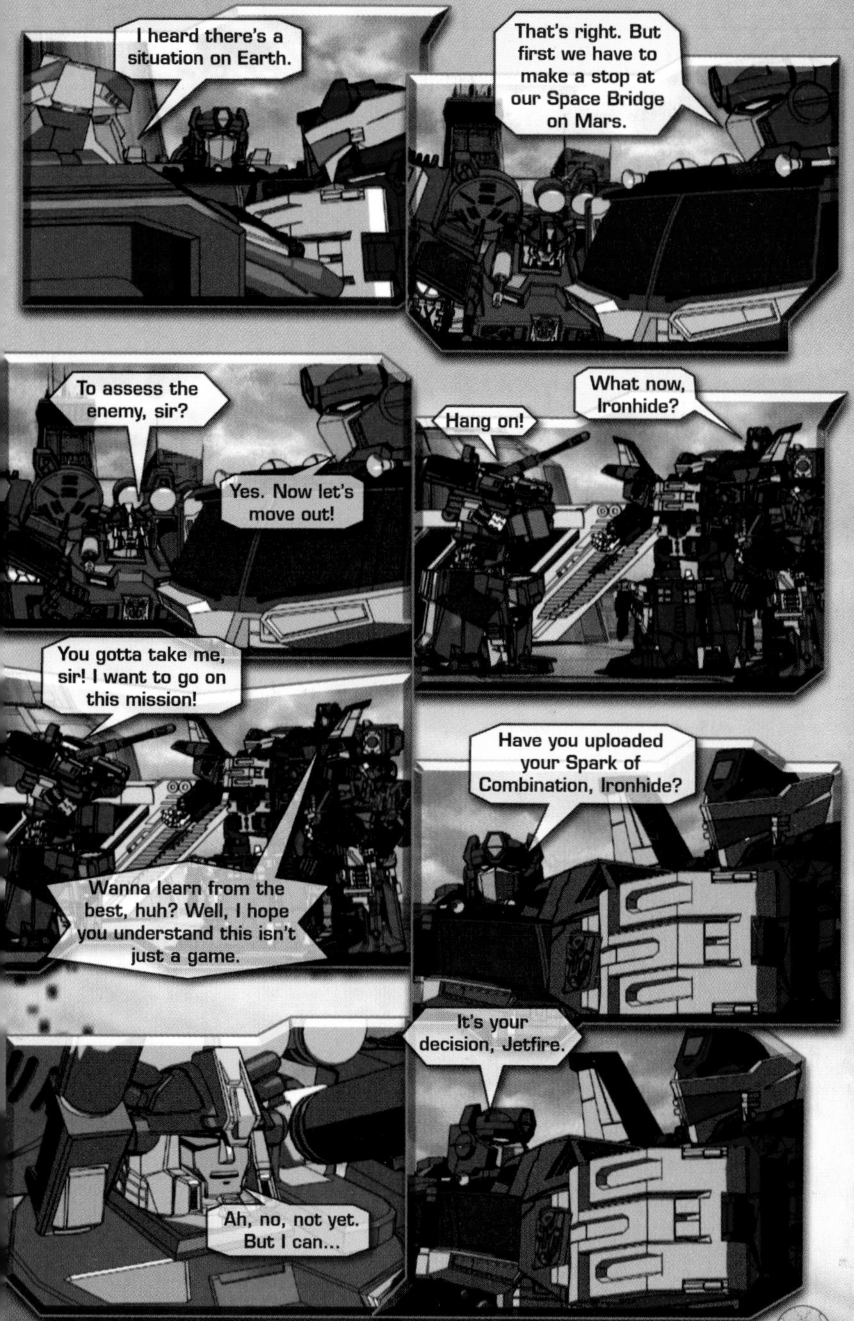
I heard there's a situation on Earth.
That's right. But first we have to make a stop at our Space Bridge on Mars.
To assess the enemy, sir?
Yes. Now let's move out!
Hang on!
What now, Ironhide?
You gotta take me, sir! I want to go on this mission!
Wanna learn from the best, huh? Well, I hope you understand this isn't just a game.
Have you uploaded your Spark of Combination, Ironhide?
Ah, no, not yet. But I can...
It's your decision, Jetfire.

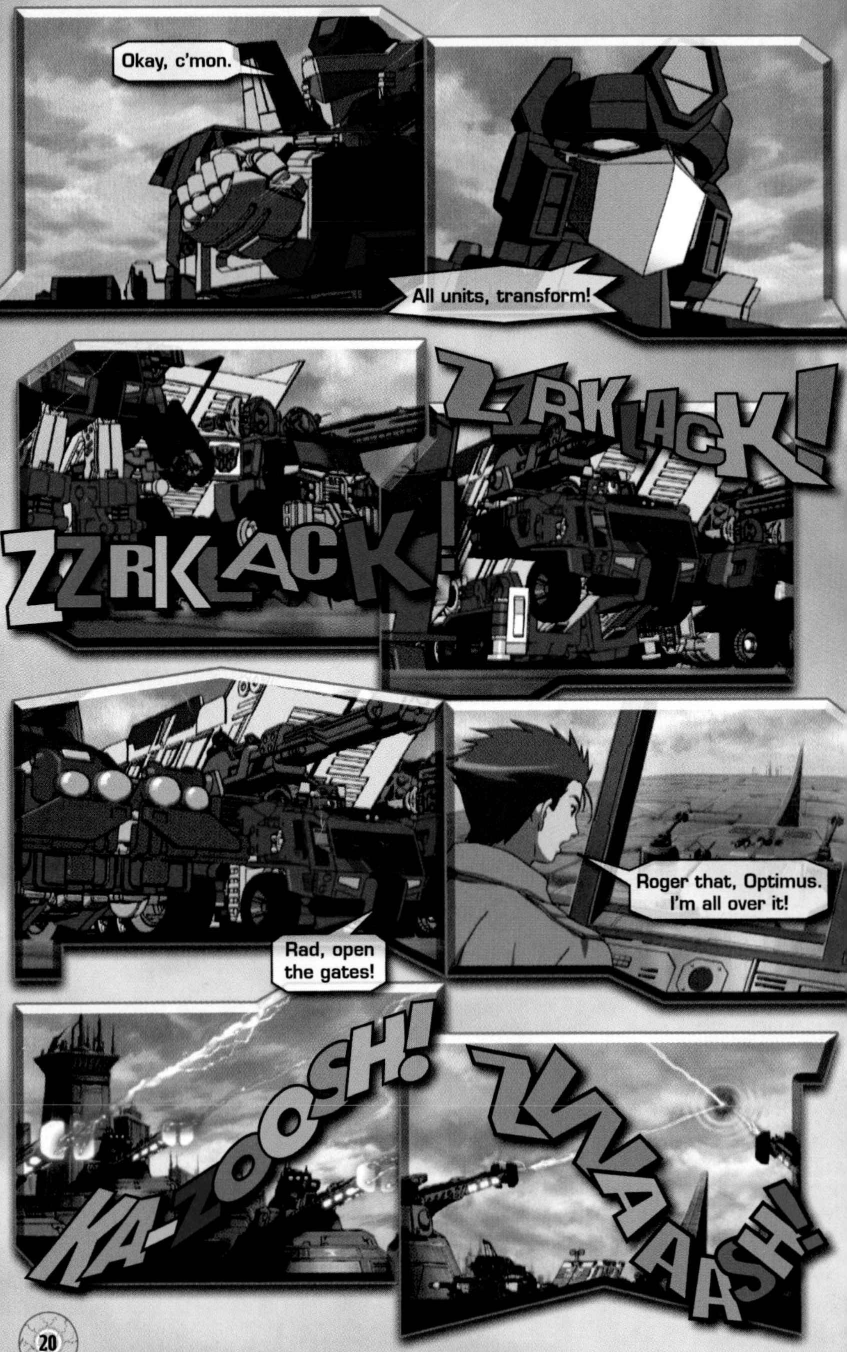
Okay, c'mon.
All units, transform!
ZZRKLACK!
ZZRKLACK!
Rad, open the gates!
Roger that, Optimus. I'm all over it!
KA-ZOOOSH!
ZZVVAAASH!

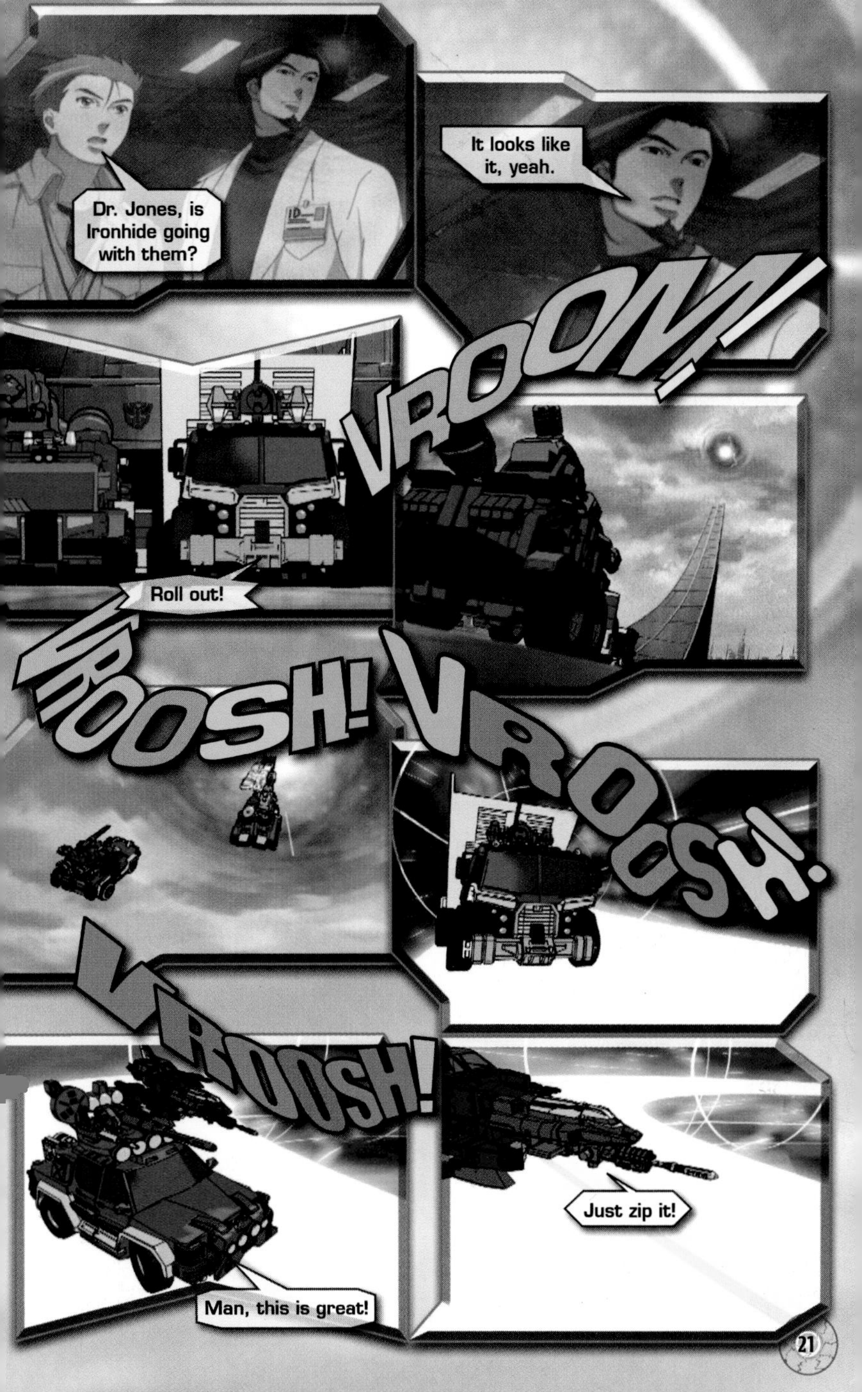
Dr. Jones, is Ironhide going with them?
It looks like it, yeah.
VROOM!
Roll out!
VROOSH!
VROOSH!
VROOSH!
Man, this is great!
Just zip it!

Planet Mars...

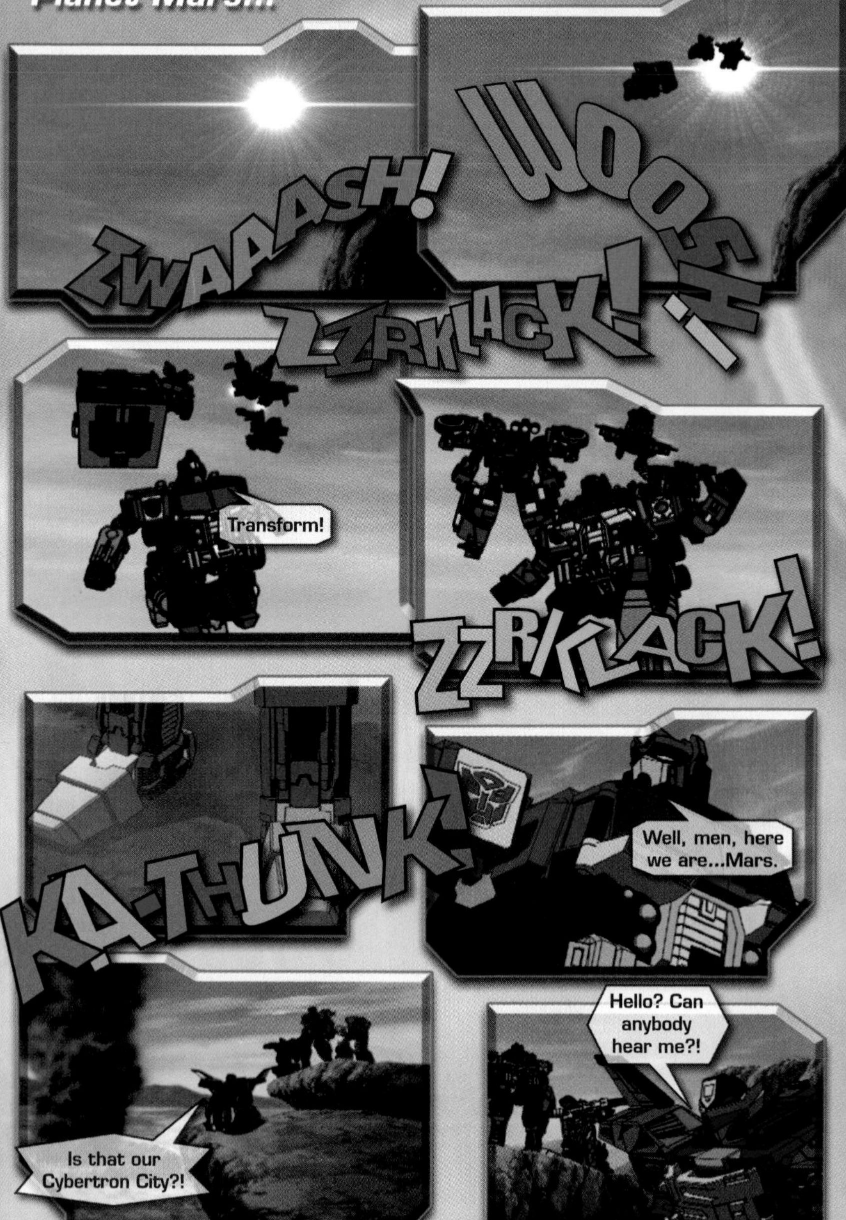
ZWAAASH!
WOOSH!
ZZRKLACK!
Transform!
ZZRKLACK!
KA-THUNK!
Well, men, here we are...Mars.
Is that our Cybertron City?!
Hello? Can anybody hear me?!

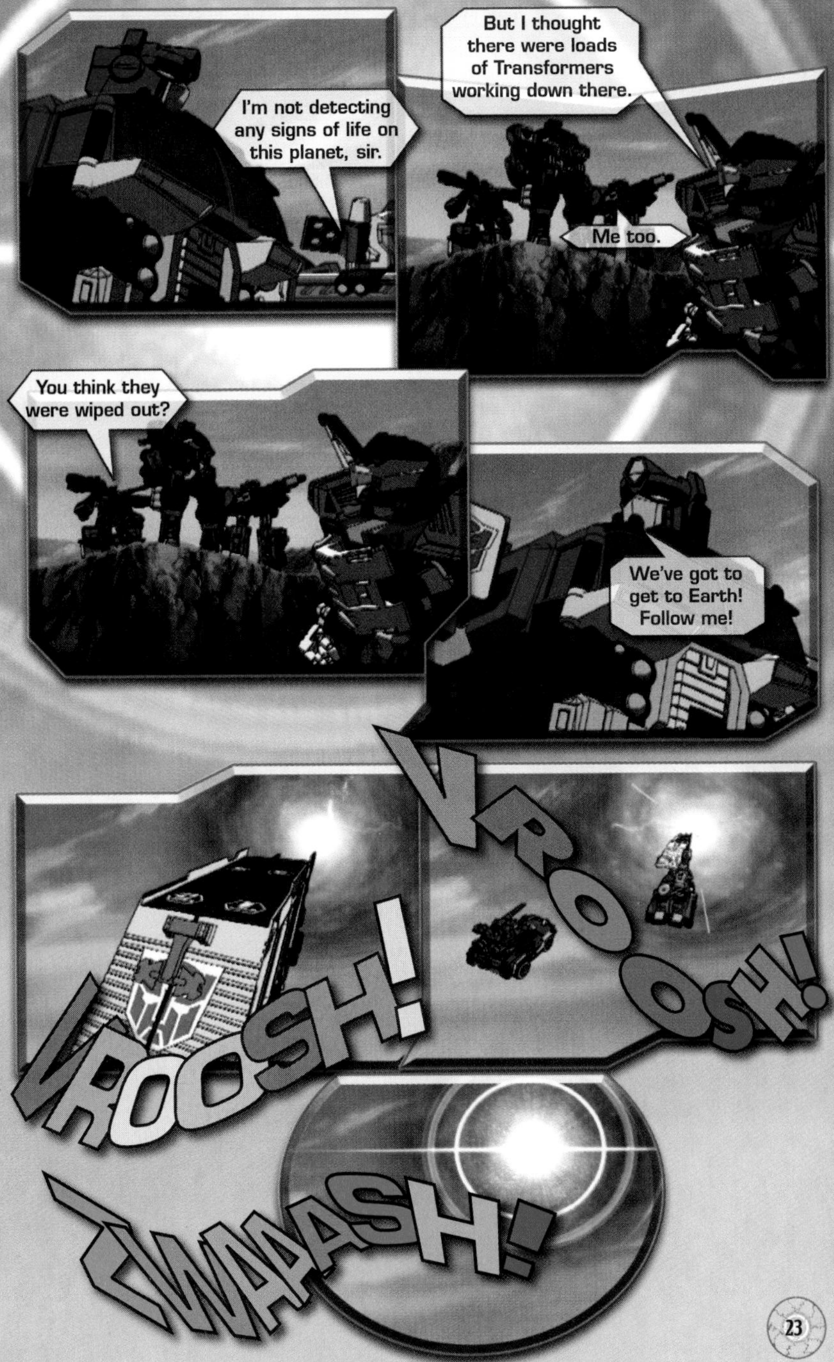
I'm not detecting any signs of life on this planet, sir.
But I thought there were loads of Transformers working down there.
Me too.
You think they were wiped out?
We've got to get to Earth! Follow me!
VROOOSH!
VROOOSH!
ZWAAASH!

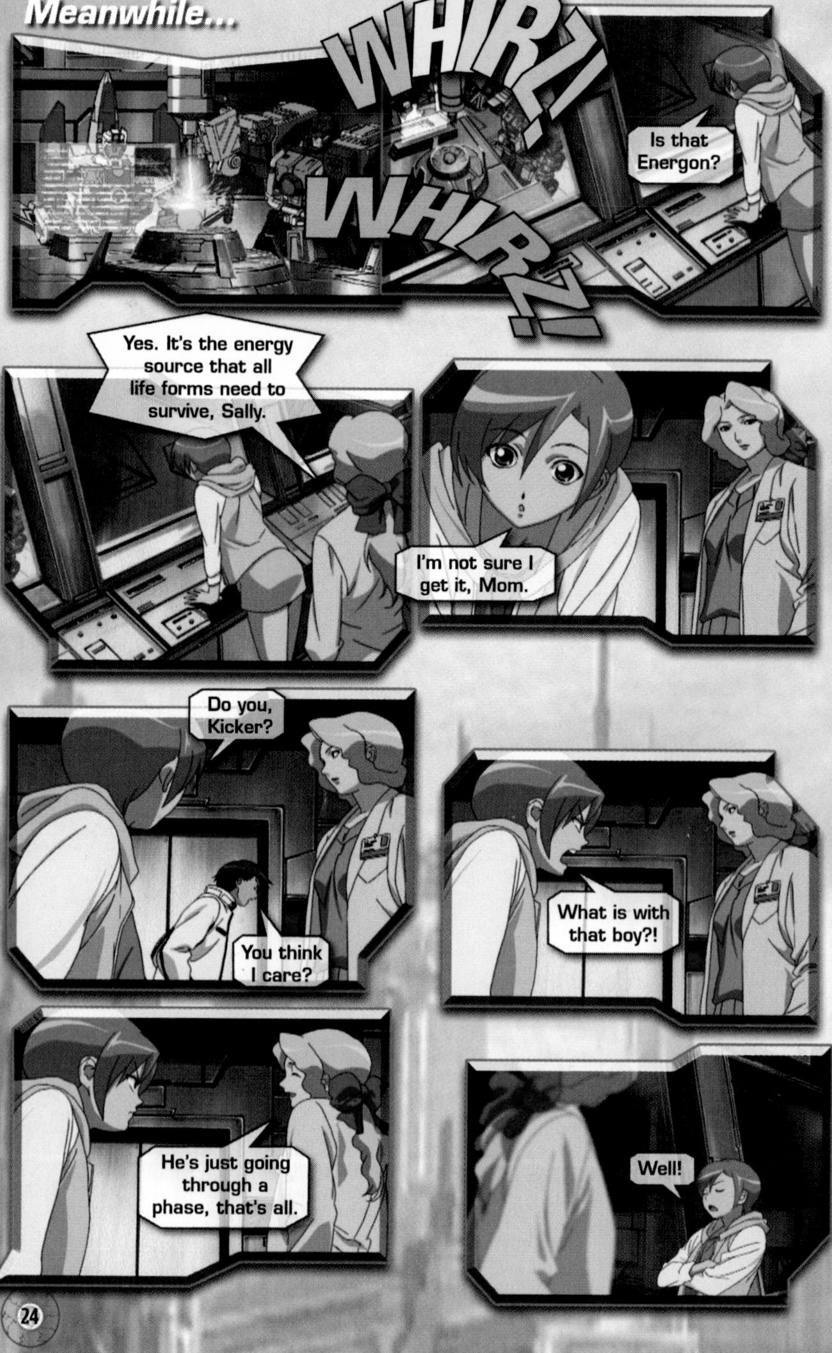
Meanwhile...
WHIRZ!
WHIRZ!
Is that Energon?
Yes. It's the energy source that all life forms need to survive, Sally.
I'm not sure I get it, Mom.
Do you, Kicker?
You think I care?
What is with that boy?!
He's just going through a phase, that's all.
Well!

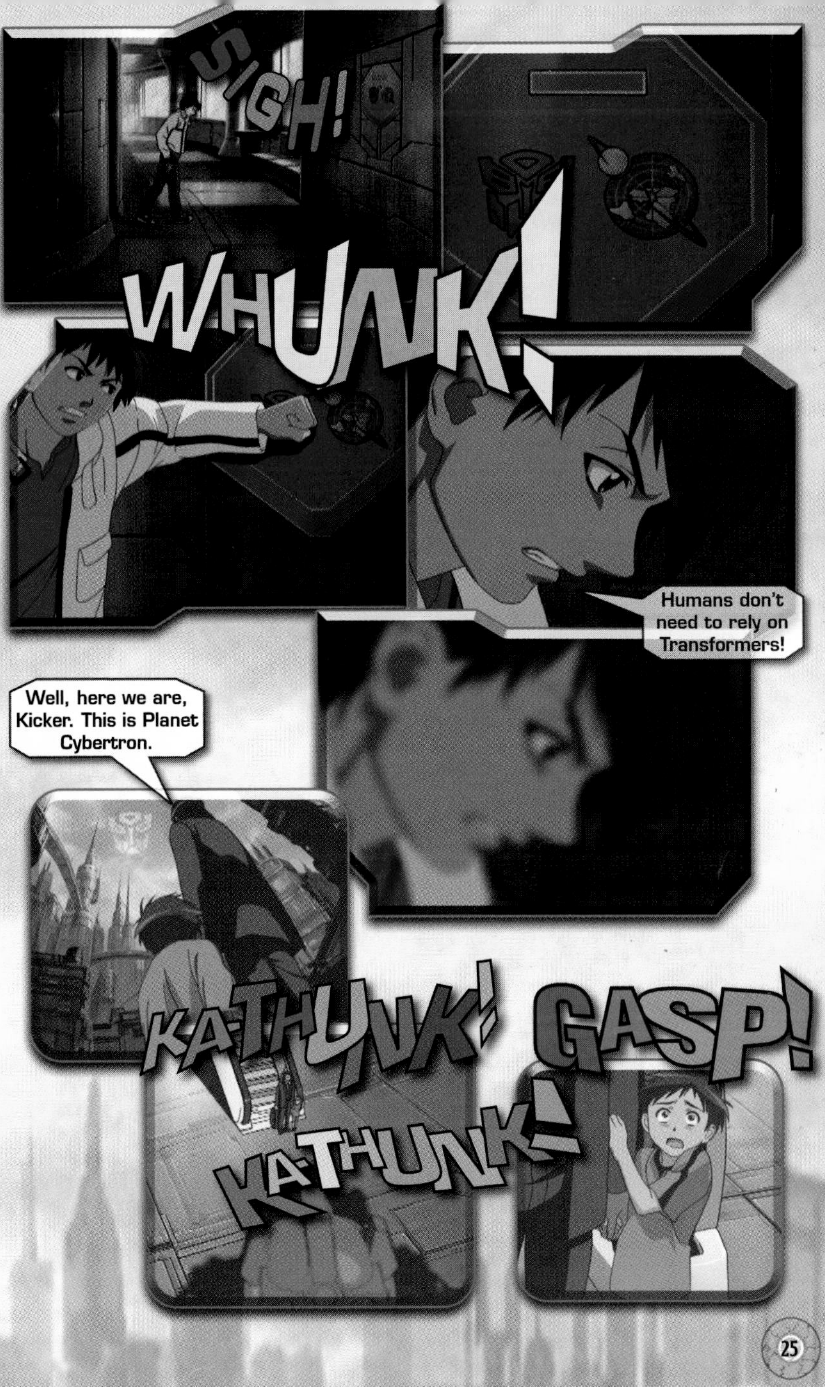
SIGH!
WHUNK!
Humans don't need to rely on Transformers!
Well, here we are, Kicker. This is Planet Cybertron.
KA-THUNK!
KA-THUNK!
GASP!

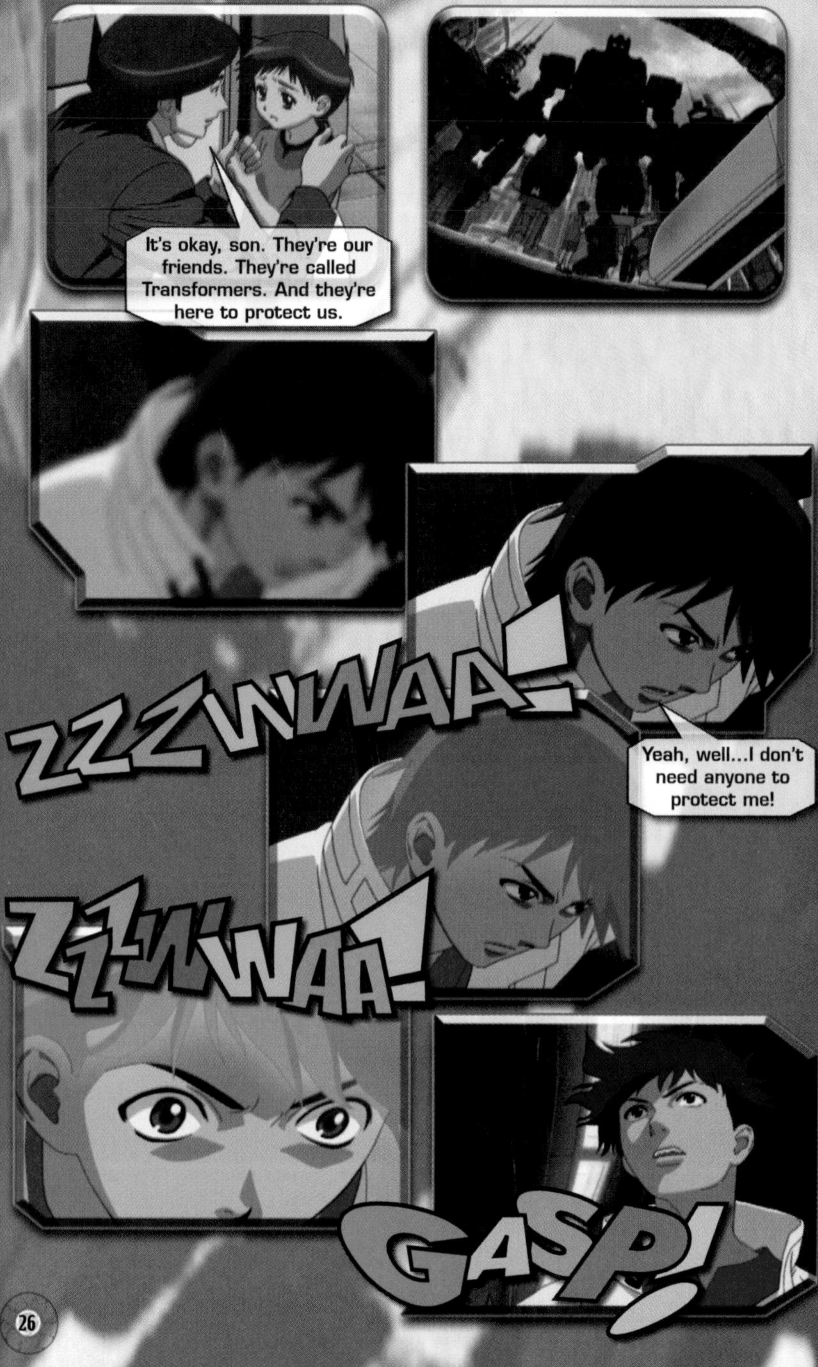
It's okay, son. They're our friends. They're called Transformers. And they're here to protect us.
ZZZWWAA!
Yeah, well...I don't need anyone to protect me!
ZZZWWAA!
GASP!

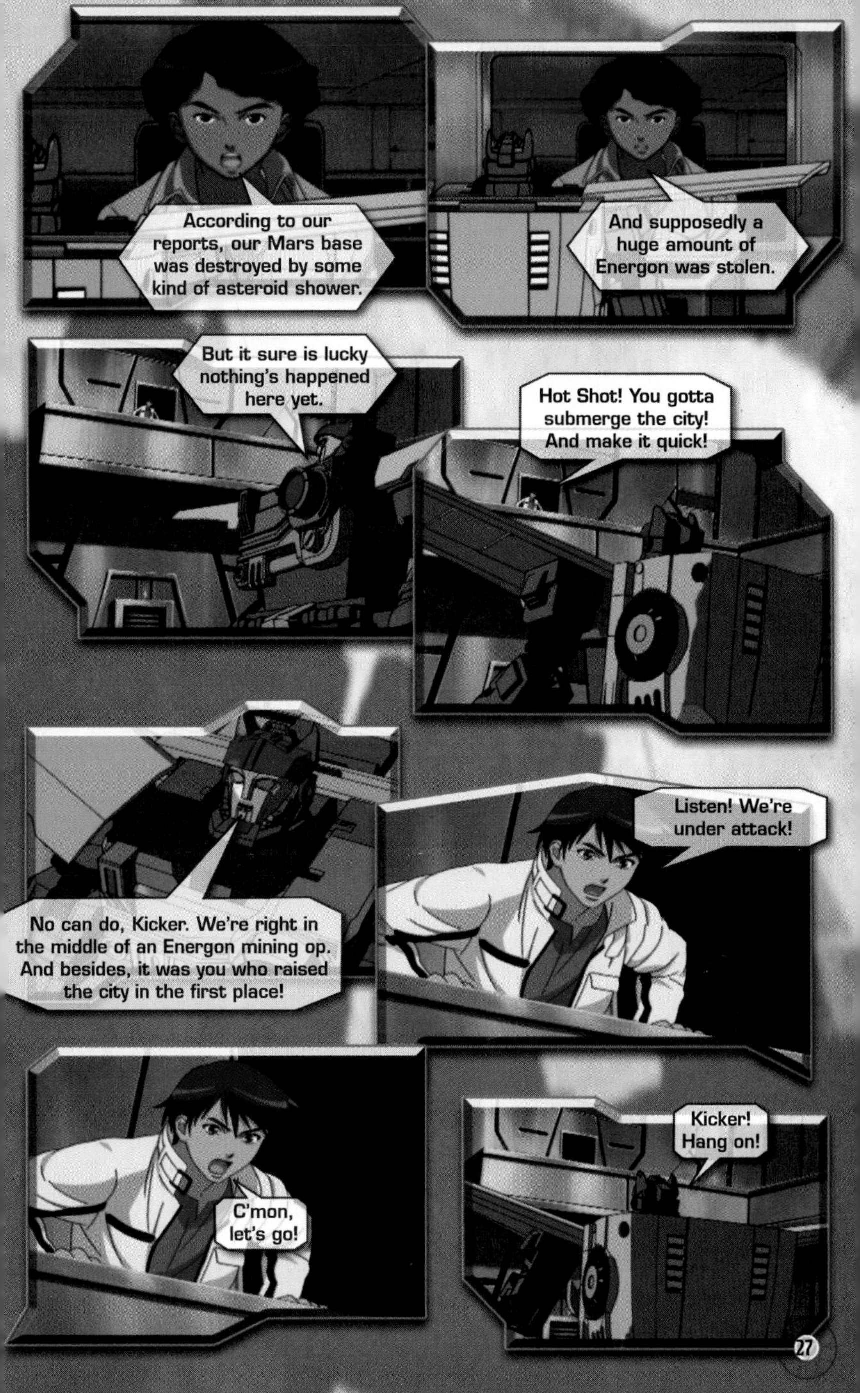
According to our reports, our Mars base was destroyed by some kind of asteroid shower.
And supposedly a huge amount of Energon was stolen.
But it sure is lucky nothing's happened here yet.
Hot Shot! You gotta submerge the city! And make it quick!
No can do, Kicker. We're right in the middle of an Energon mining op. And besides, it was you who raised the city in the first place!
Listen! We're under attack!
C'mon, let's go!
Kicker! Hang on!

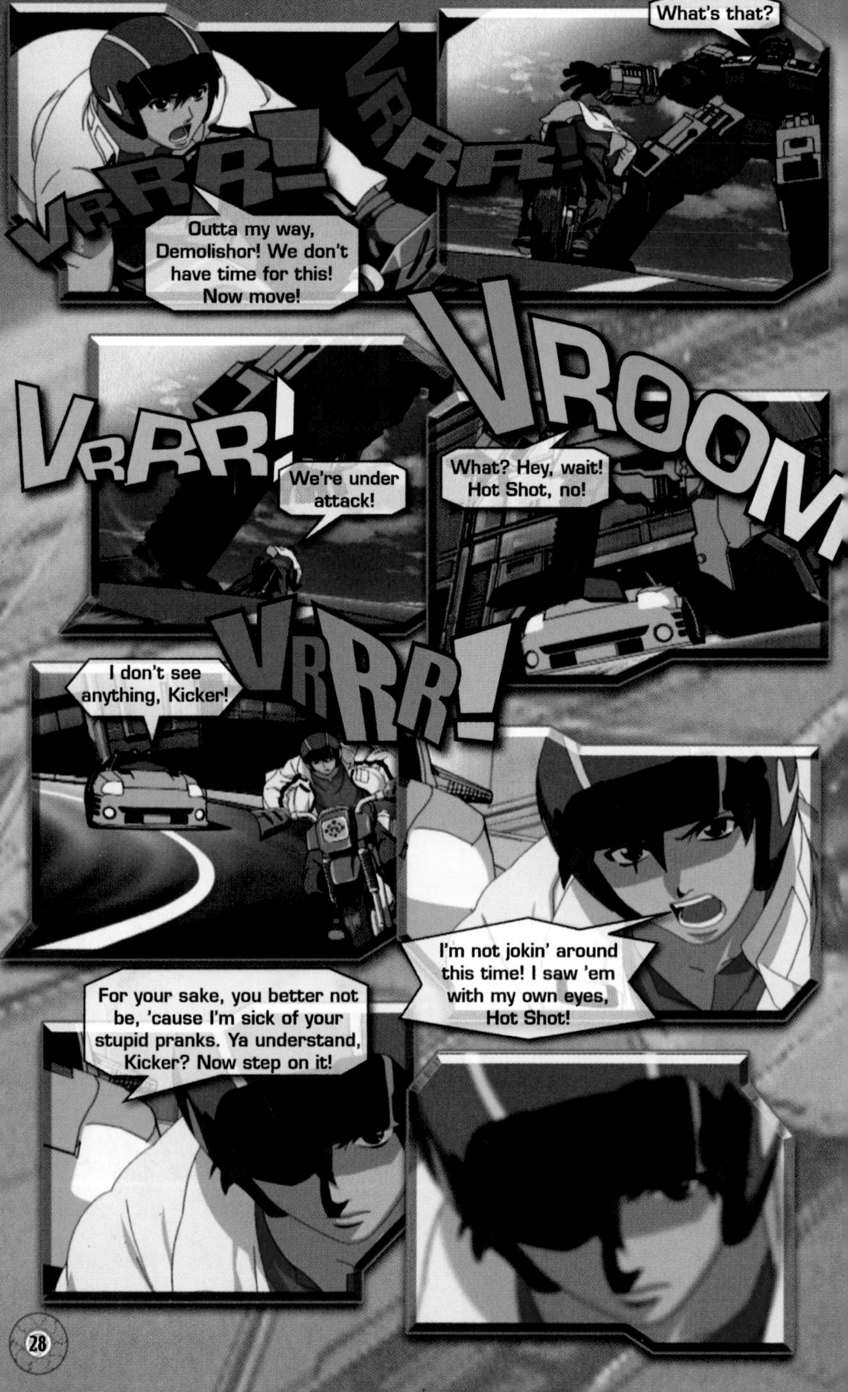
VRRRA!
Outta my way, Demolishor! We don't have time for this! Now move!
VRRRA!
What's that?
VRRR!
We're under attack!
VROOM!
What? Hey, wait! Hot Shot, no!
VRRR!
I don't see anything, Kicker!
I'm not jokin' around this time! I saw 'em with my own eyes, Hot Shot!
For your sake, you better not be, 'cause I'm sick of your stupid pranks. Ya understand, Kicker? Now step on it!

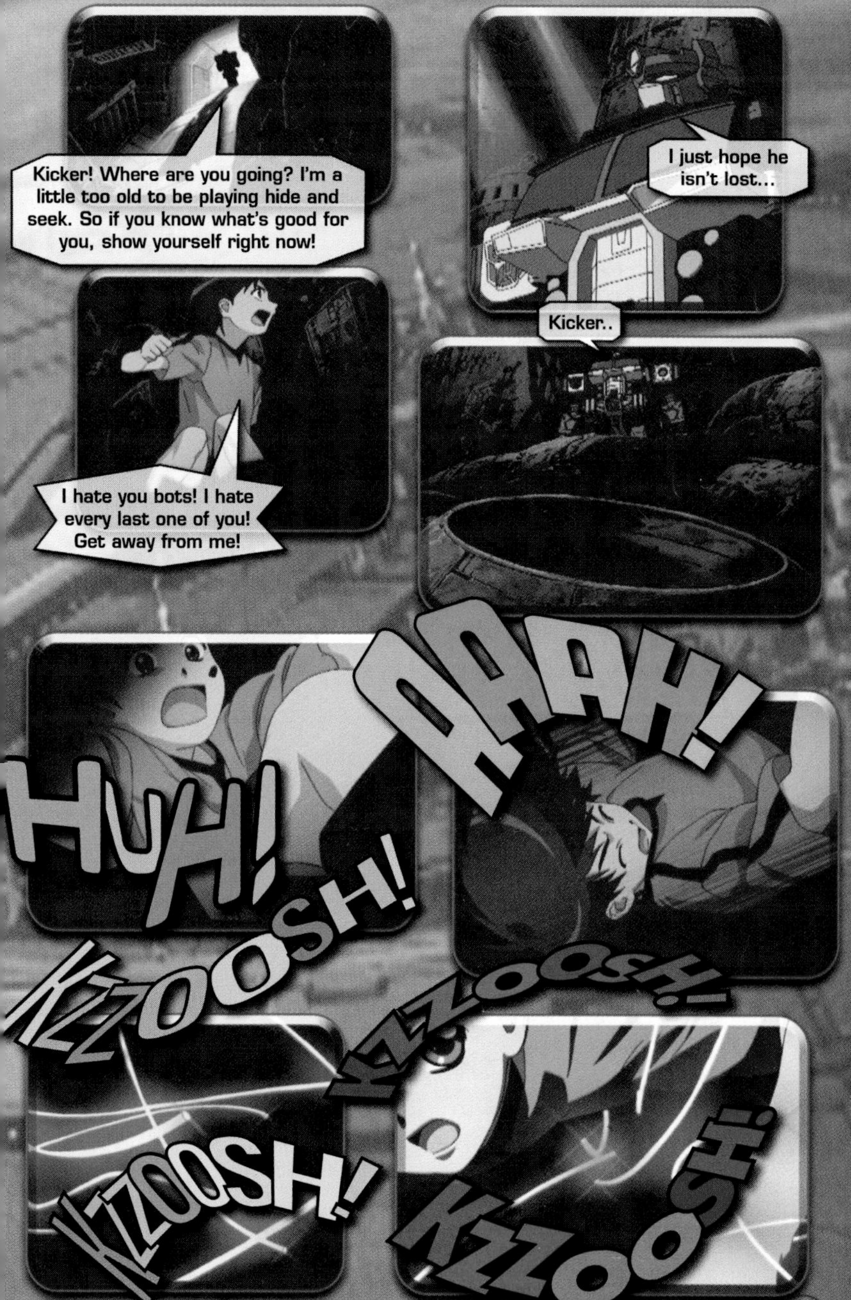
Kicker! Where are you going? I'm a little too old to be playing hide and seek. So if you know what's good for you, show yourself right now!
I just hope he isn't lost...
I hate you bots! I hate every last one of you! Get away from me!
Kicker..
HUH!
AAAH!
KZZOOSH!
KZZOOSH!
KZZOOSH!
KZZOOSH!

GASP!

What happened?

So, you're the one who discovered me...

I find you humans interesting creatures, and I'm curious what type of energy source you rely on.

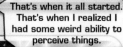

KA-THUNK!

That's when it all started. That's when I realized I had some weird ability to perceive things.

What's going on here?!

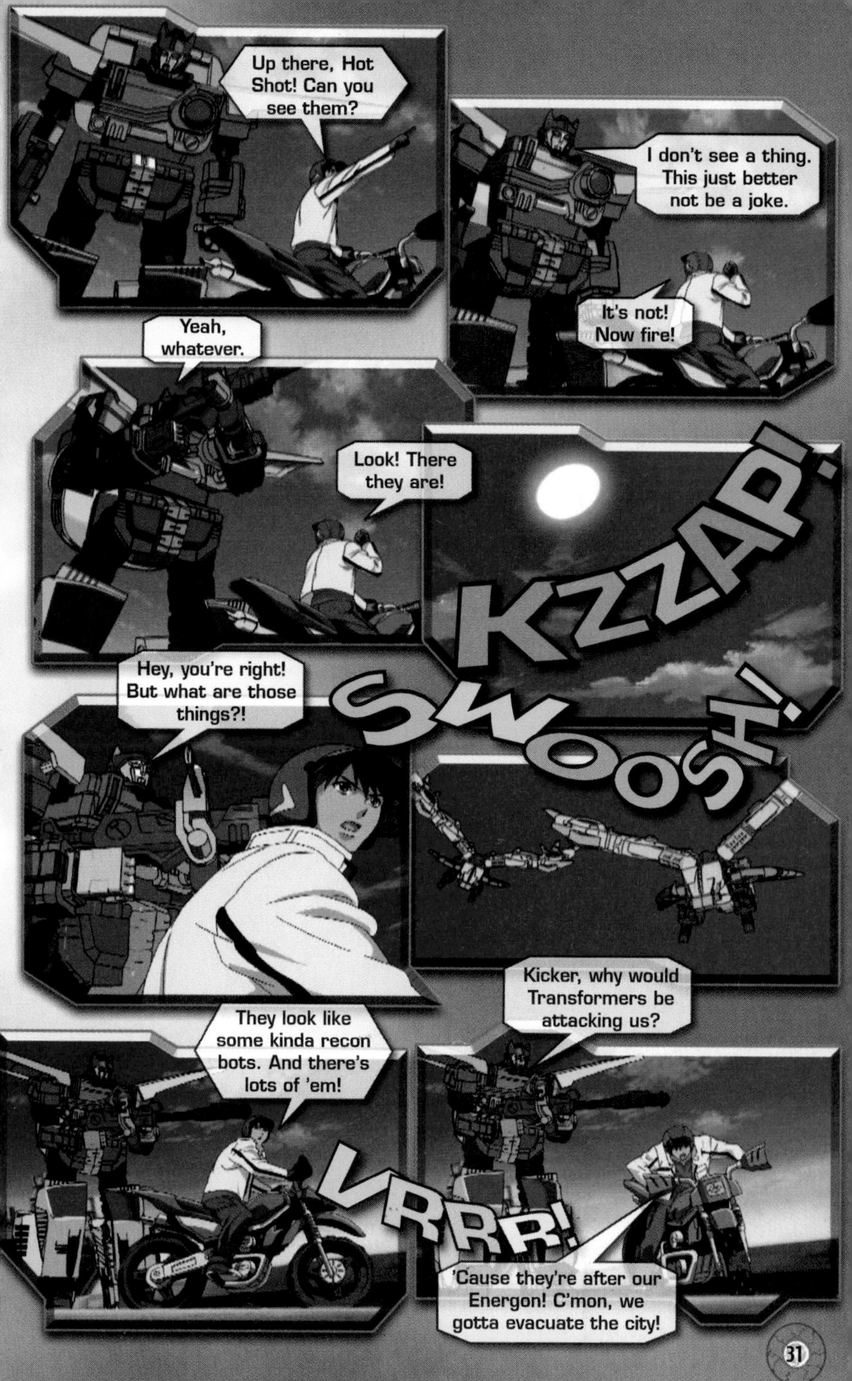
Up there, Hot Shot! Can you see them?
I don't see a thing. This just better not be a joke.
It's not! Now fire!
Yeah, whatever.
Look! There they are!
KZZAP!
Hey, you're right! But what are those things?!
SWOOSH!
They look like some kinda recon bots. And there's lots of 'em!
VRRR!
Kicker, why would Transformers be attacking us?
'Cause they're after our Energon! C'mon, we gotta evacuate the city!

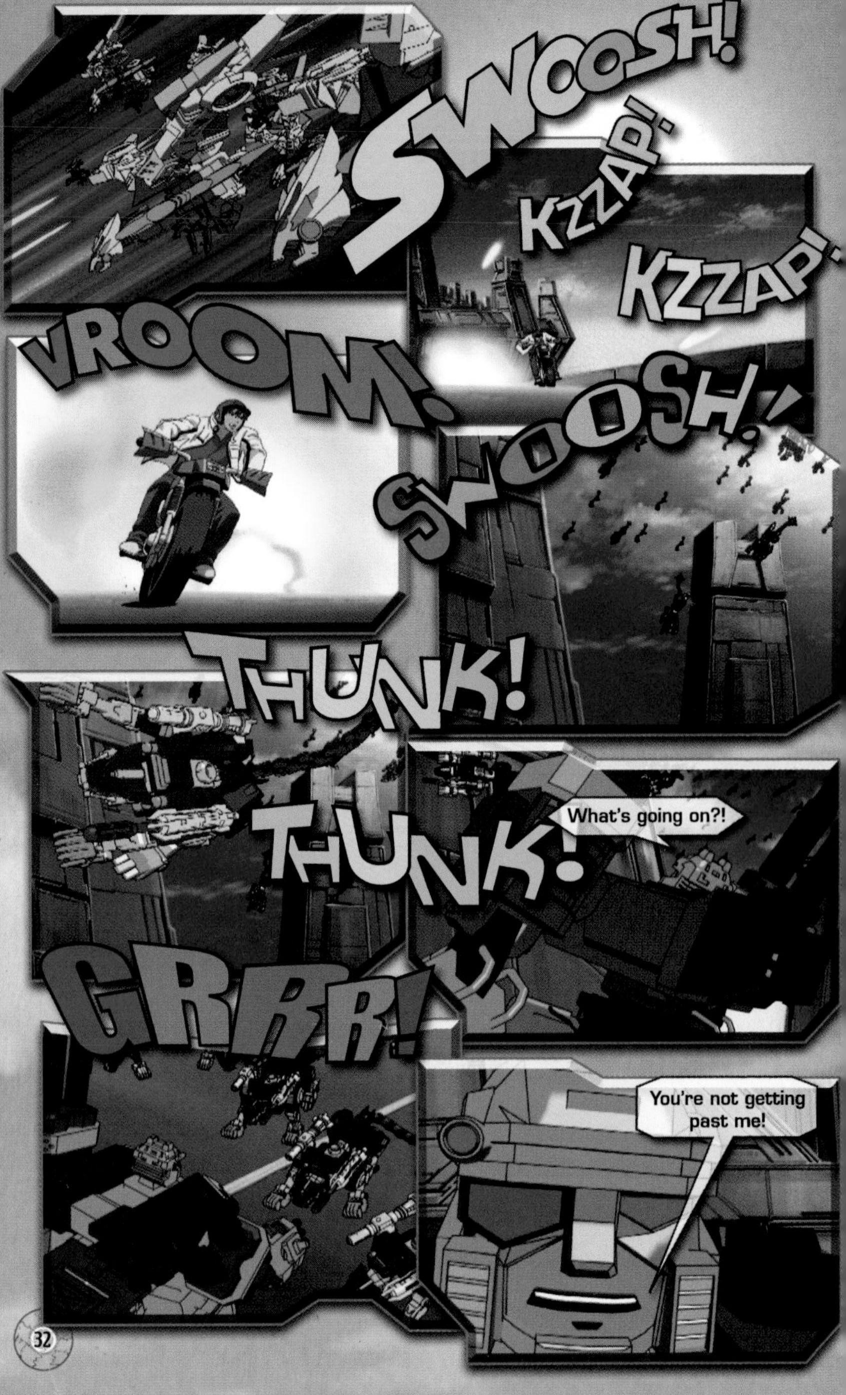
SWOOSH!
KZZAP!
KZZAP!
VROOM!
SWOOSH!
THUNK!
THUNK!
What's going on?!
GRRR!
You're not getting past me!

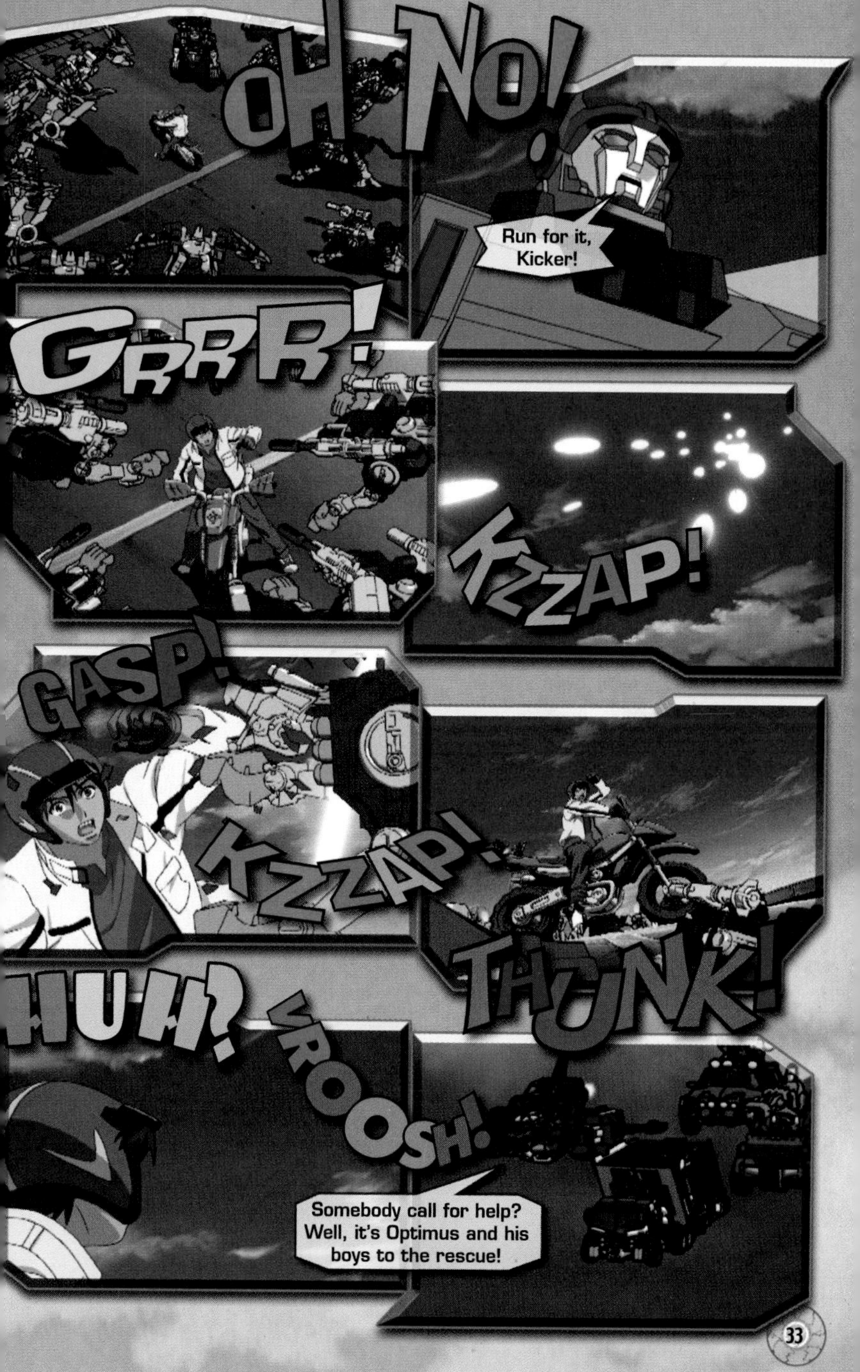
OH NO!
Run for it, Kicker!
GRRR!
KZZAP!
GASP!
KZZAP!
THUNK!
HUH?
VROOSH!
Somebody call for help? Well, it's Optimus and his boys to the rescue!

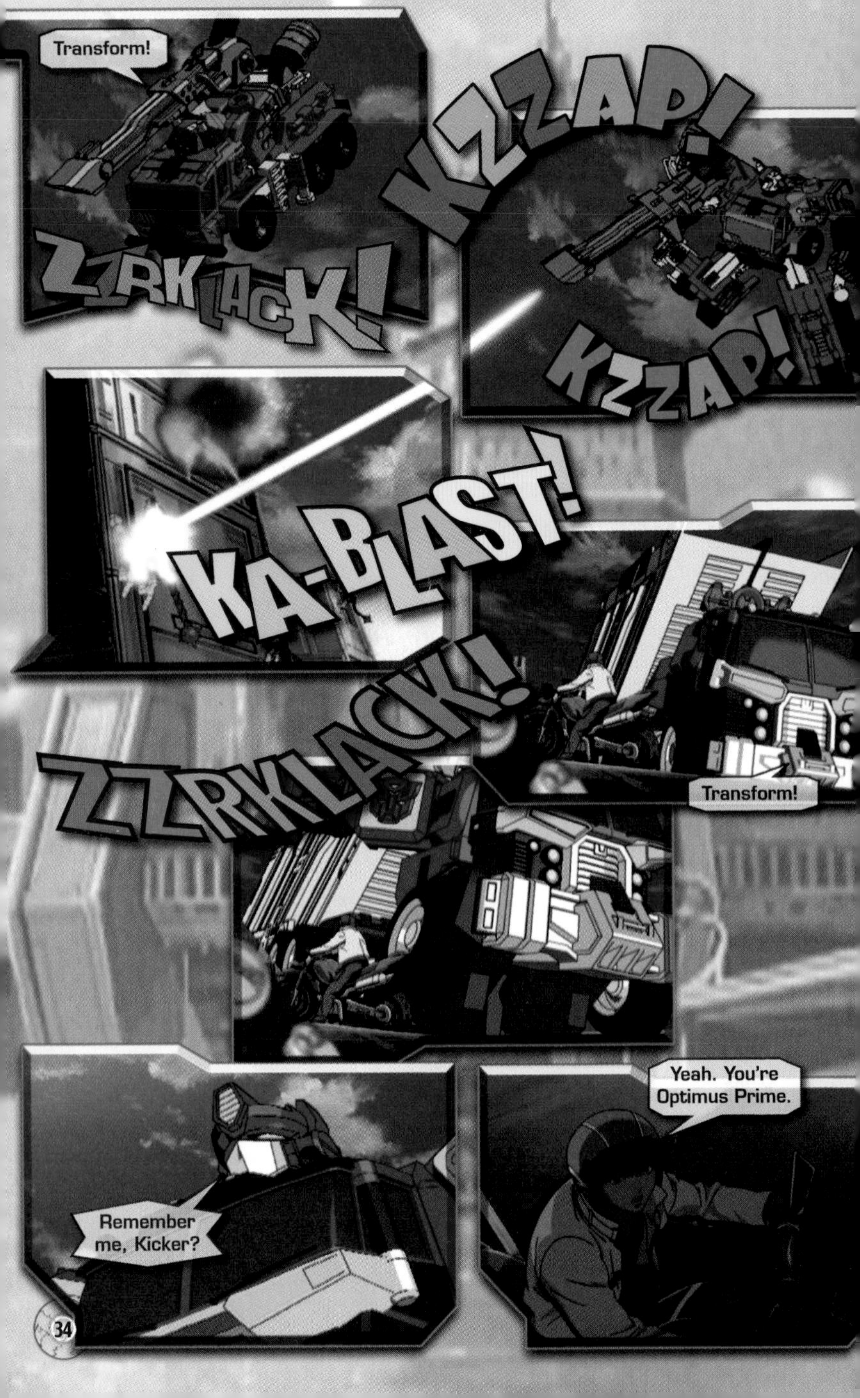

Transform!
ZZRKLACK!
KZZAP!
KZZAP!
KA-BLAST!
Transform!
ZZRKLACK!
Remember me, Kicker?
Yeah. You're Optimus Prime.

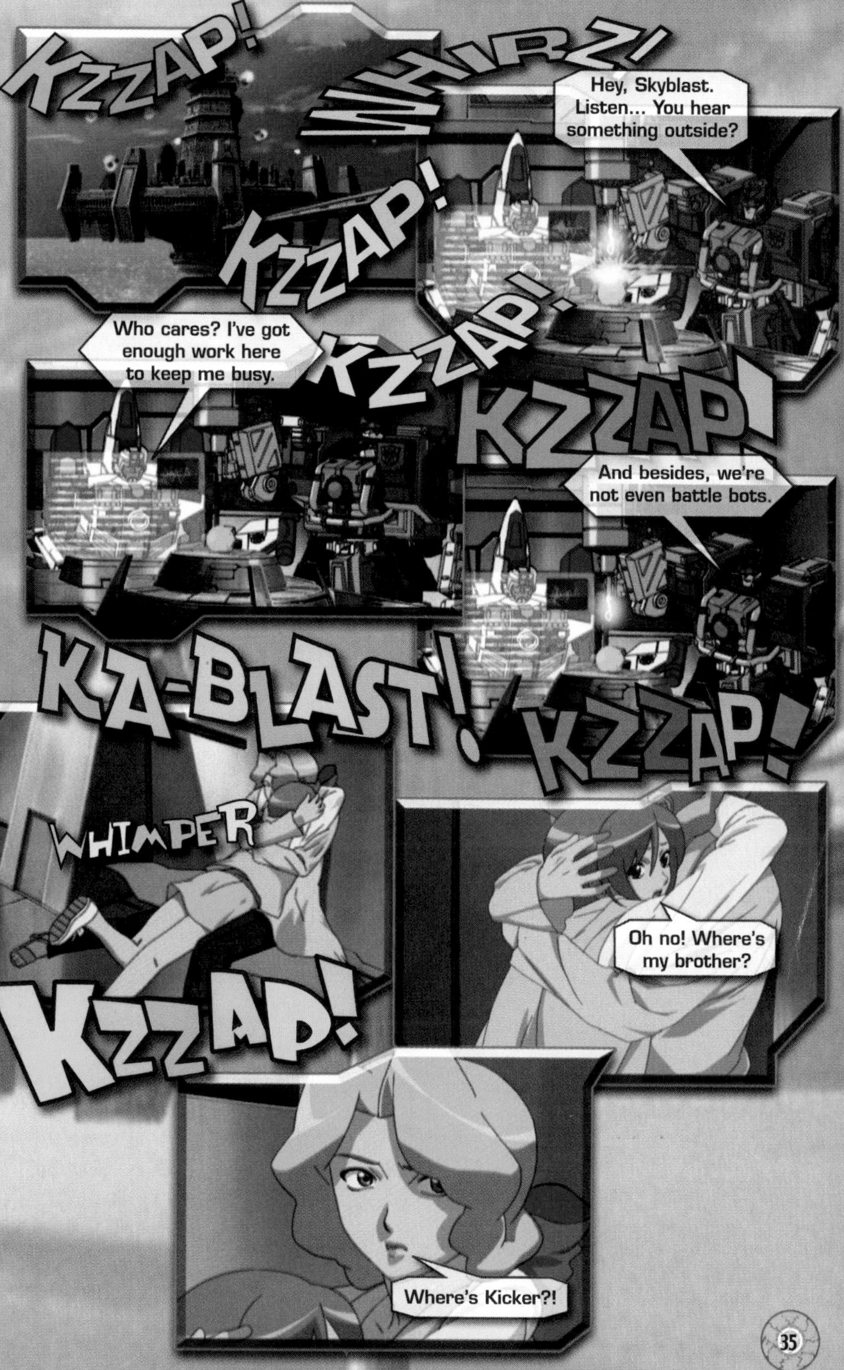
KZZAP!
WHIRZ!
Hey, Skyblast. Listen... You hear something outside?
KZZAP!
KZZAP!
Who cares? I've got enough work here to keep me busy.
KZZAP!
And besides, we're not even battle bots.
KA-BLAST!
KZZAP!
WHIMPER
KZZAP!
Oh no! Where's my brother?
Where's Kicker?!

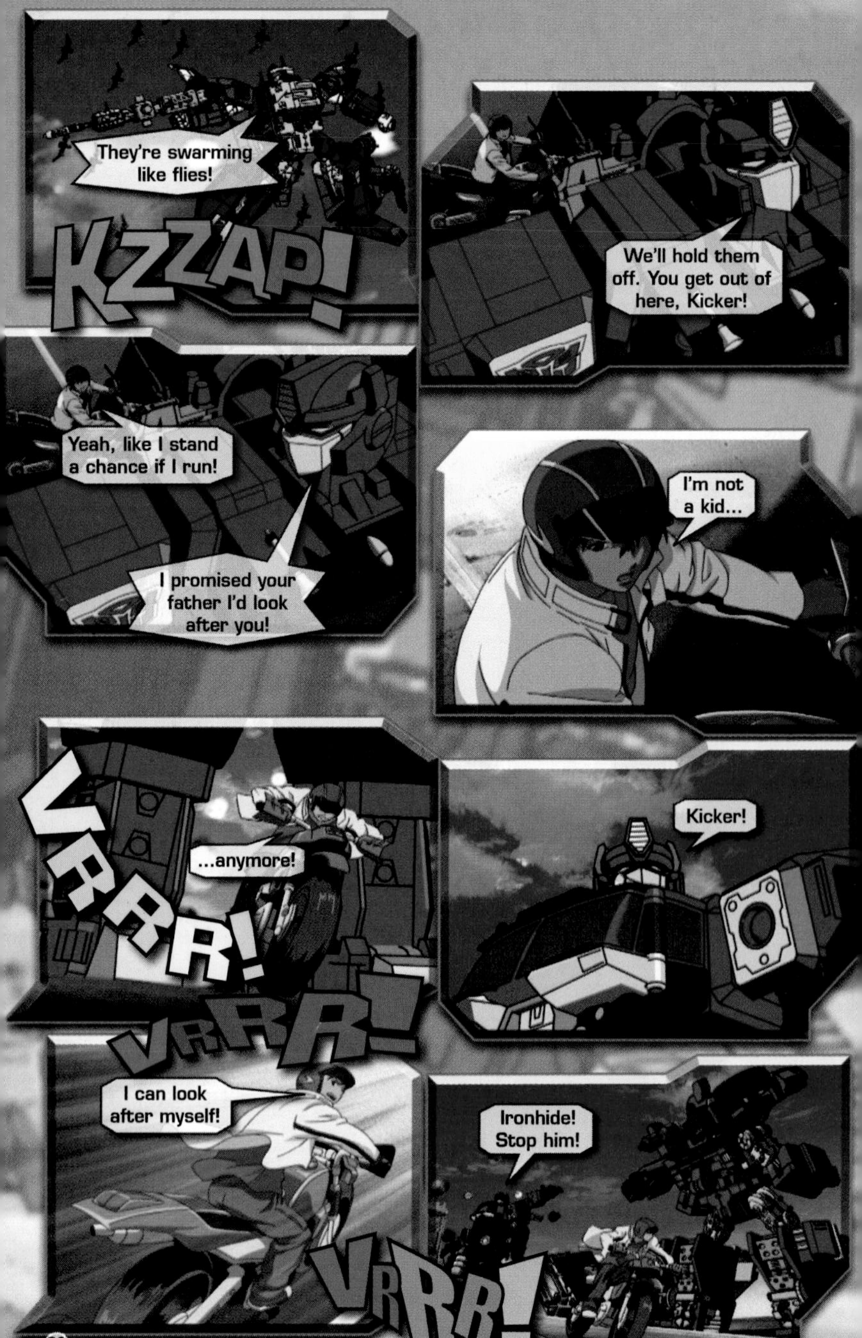
They're swarming like flies!
KZZAP!
We'll hold them off. You get out of here, Kicker!
Yeah, like I stand a chance if I run!
I promised your father I'd look after you!
I'm not a kid...
...anymore!
VRRR!
Kicker!
VRRR!
I can look after myself!
Ironhide! Stop him!
VRRR!

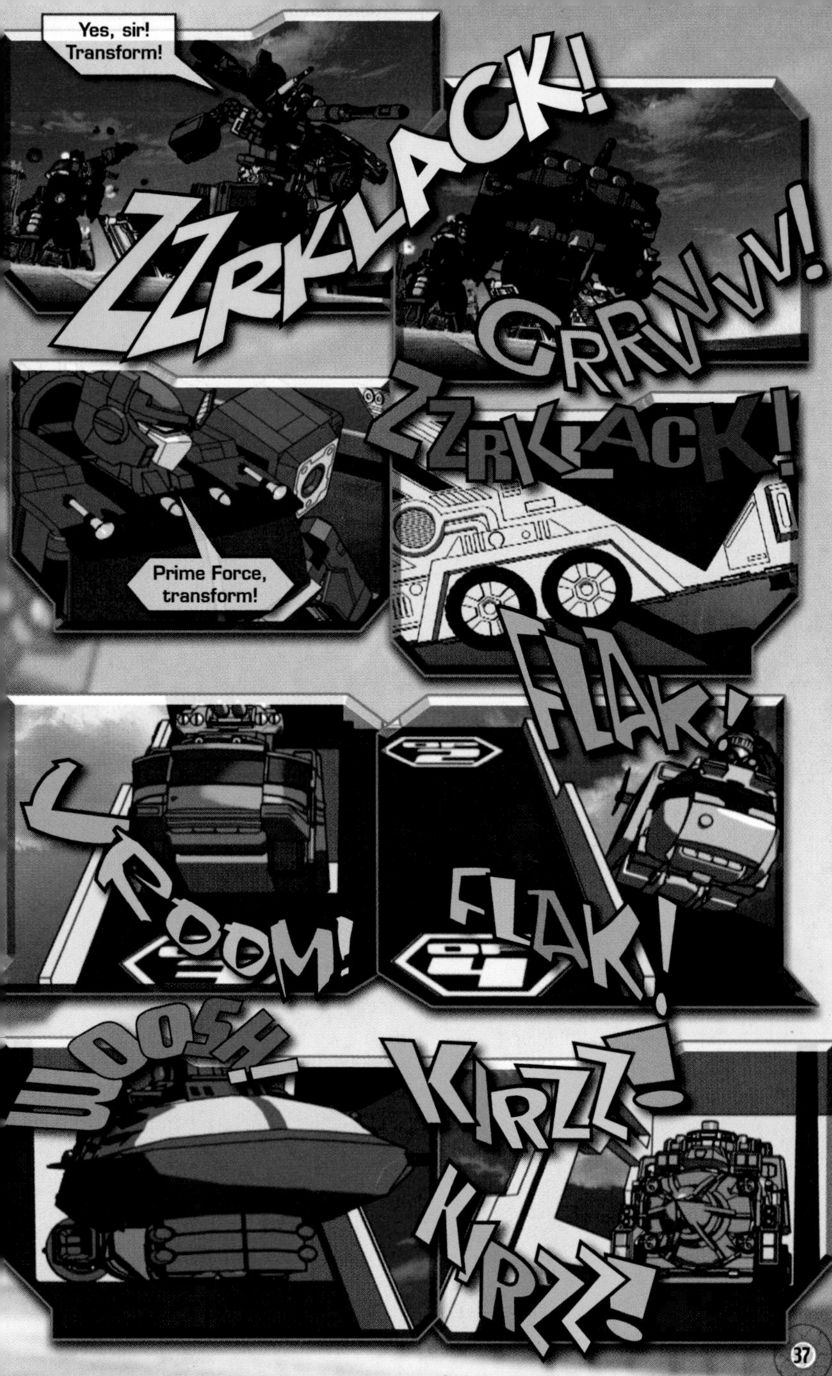
Yes, sir! Transform!
ZZRKLACK!
GRRVVVV!
Prime Force, transform!
ZZRKLACK!
FLAK!
VROOM!
FLAK!
WOOSH...
KIRZZZ-
KIRZZZ-

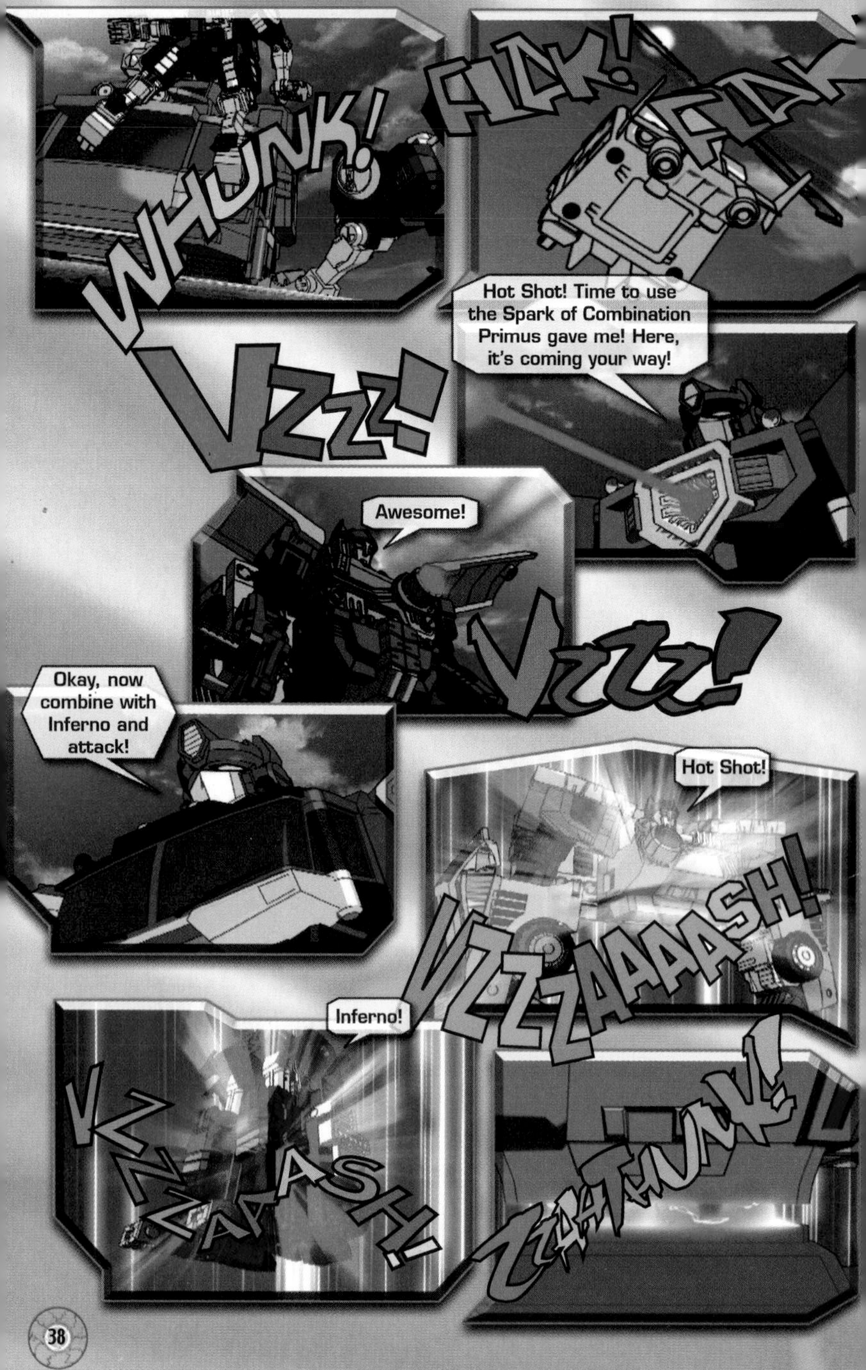
WHUNK!
Hot Shot! Time to use the Spark of Combination Primus gave me! Here, it's coming your way!
VZZZ!
Awesome!
VZZZZ!
Okay, now combine with Inferno and attack!
Hot Shot!
VZZAAAASH!
Inferno!

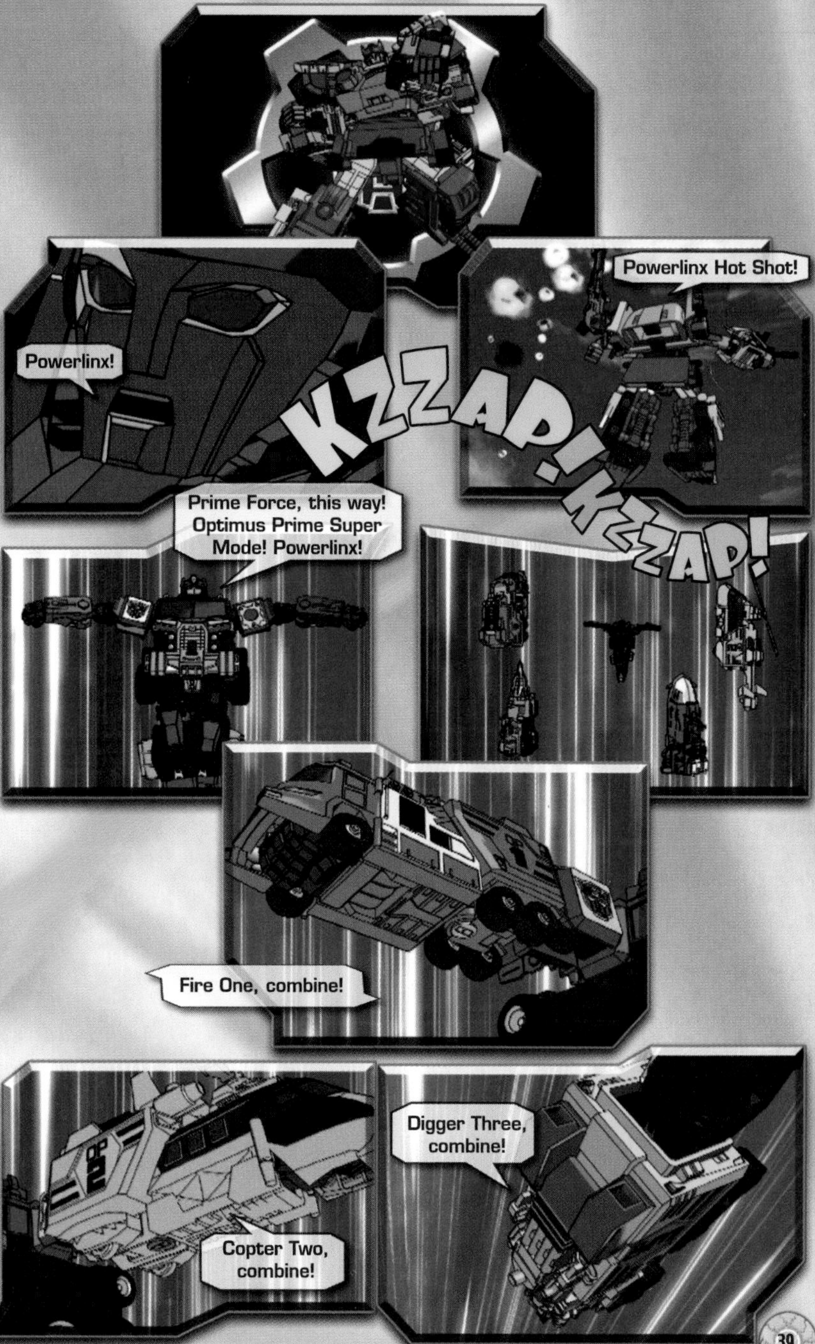
Powerlinx!
Powerlinx Hot Shot!
KZZAP! KZZAP!
Prime Force, this way! Optimus Prime Super Mode! Powerlinx!
Fire One, combine!
Copter Two, combine!
Digger Three, combine!

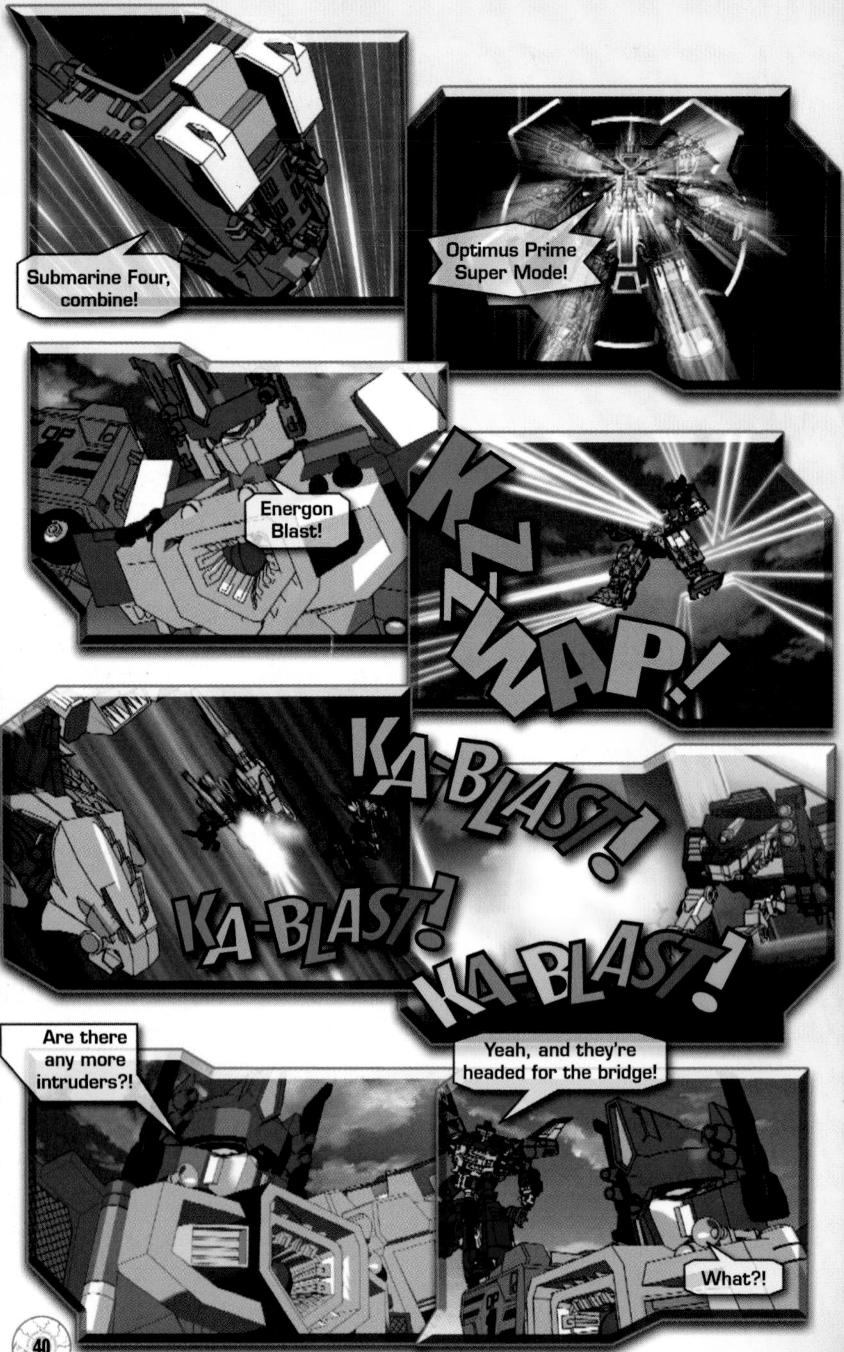
Submarine Four, combine!
Optimus Prime Super Mode!
Energon Blast!
KZZWAP!
KA-BLAST!
KA-BLAST!
KA-BLAST!
Are there any more intruders?!
Yeah, and they're headed for the bridge!
What?!

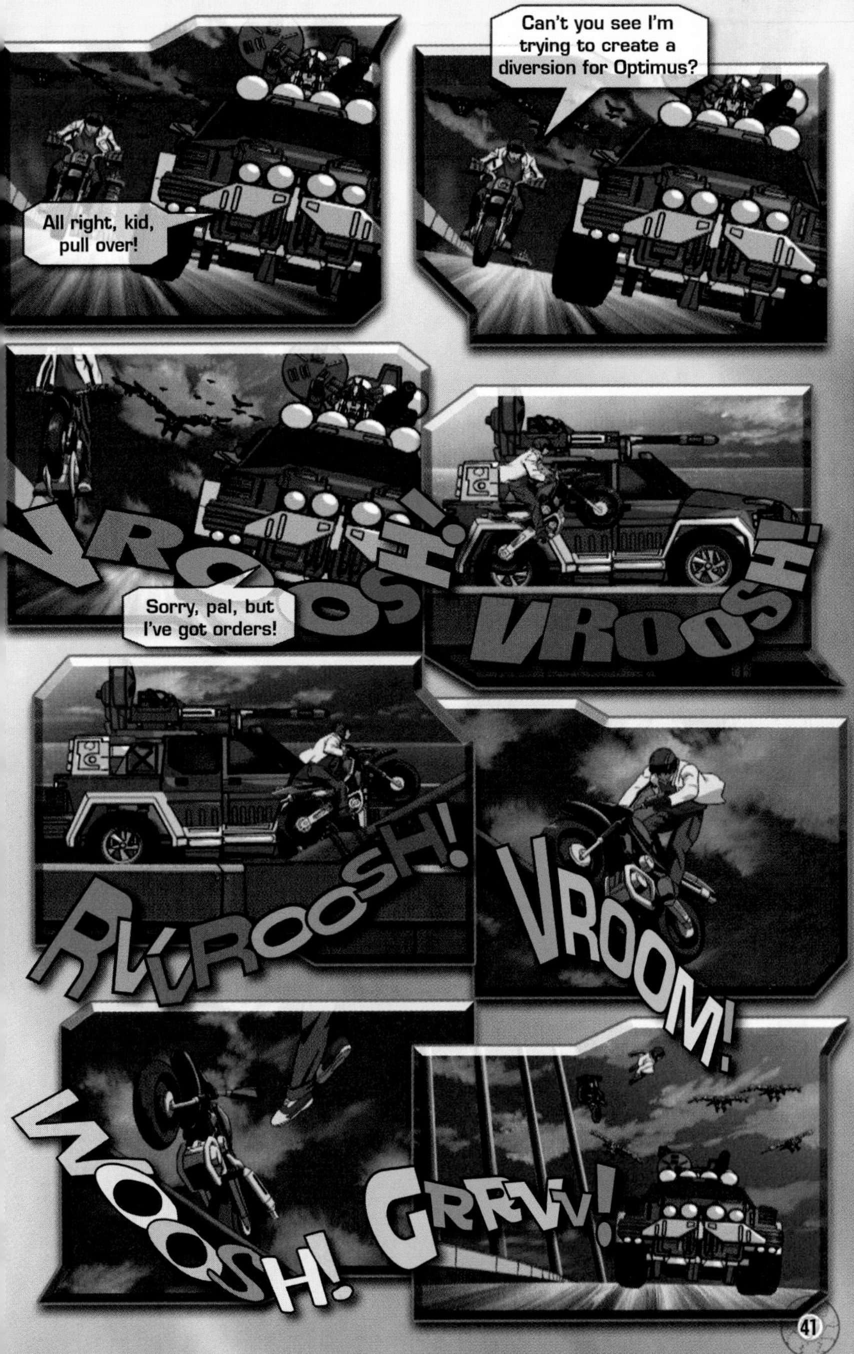
All right, kid, pull over!
Can't you see I'm trying to create a diversion for Optimus?
VROOSH!
Sorry, pal, but I've got orders!
VROOSH
RVVROOOSH!
VROOM!
WOOOSH!
GRRVVV!

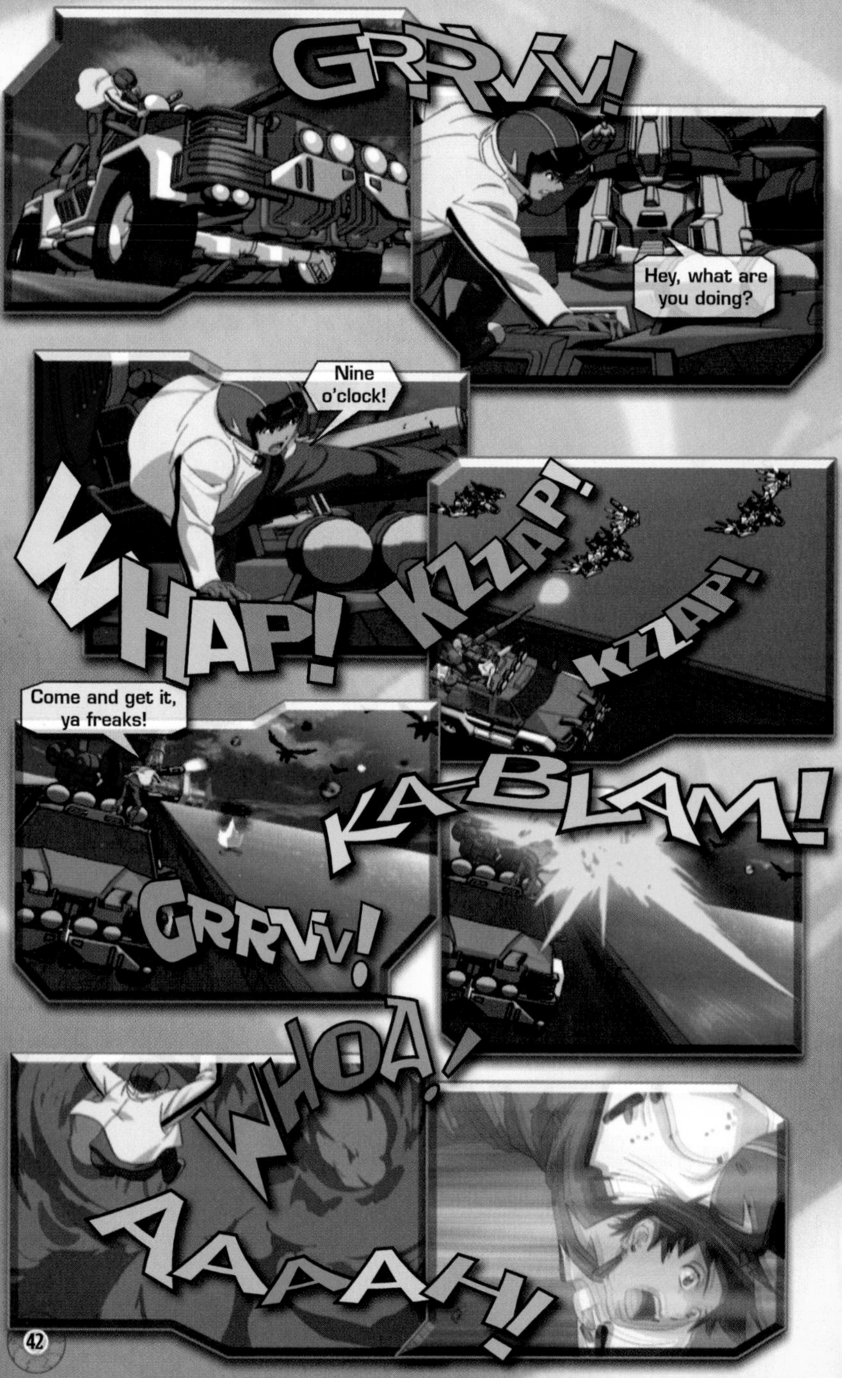
GRRVVV!
Hey, what are you doing?
Nine o'clock!
WHAP!
KZZAP!
KZZAP!
Come and get it, ya freaks!
GRRVVV!
KA-BLAM!
WHOA!
AAAAH!

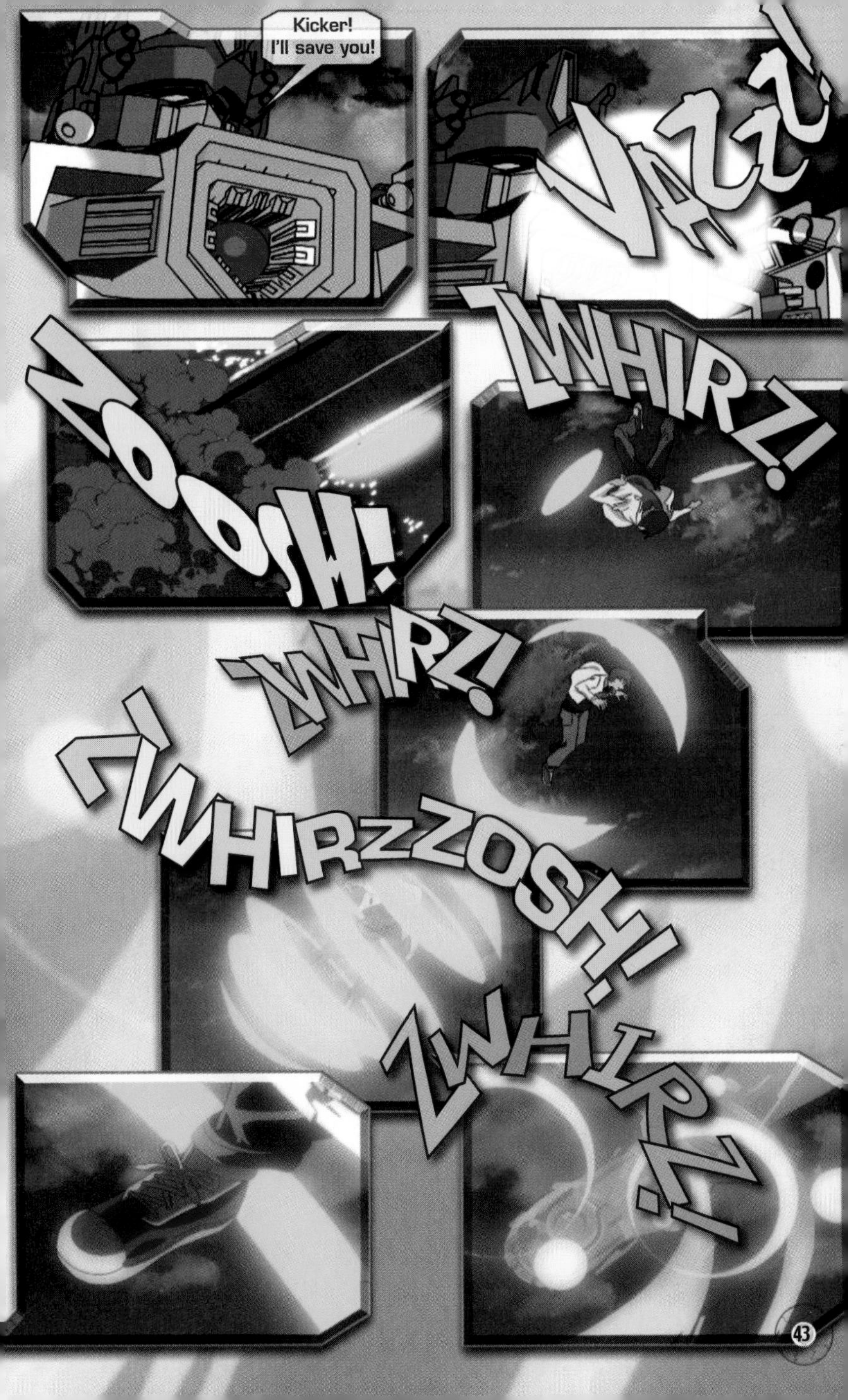
Kicker!
I'll save you!
VAZZ!
ZOOOSH!
ZWHIRZ!
ZWHIRZ!
ZWHIRZZOSH!
ZWHIRZ!

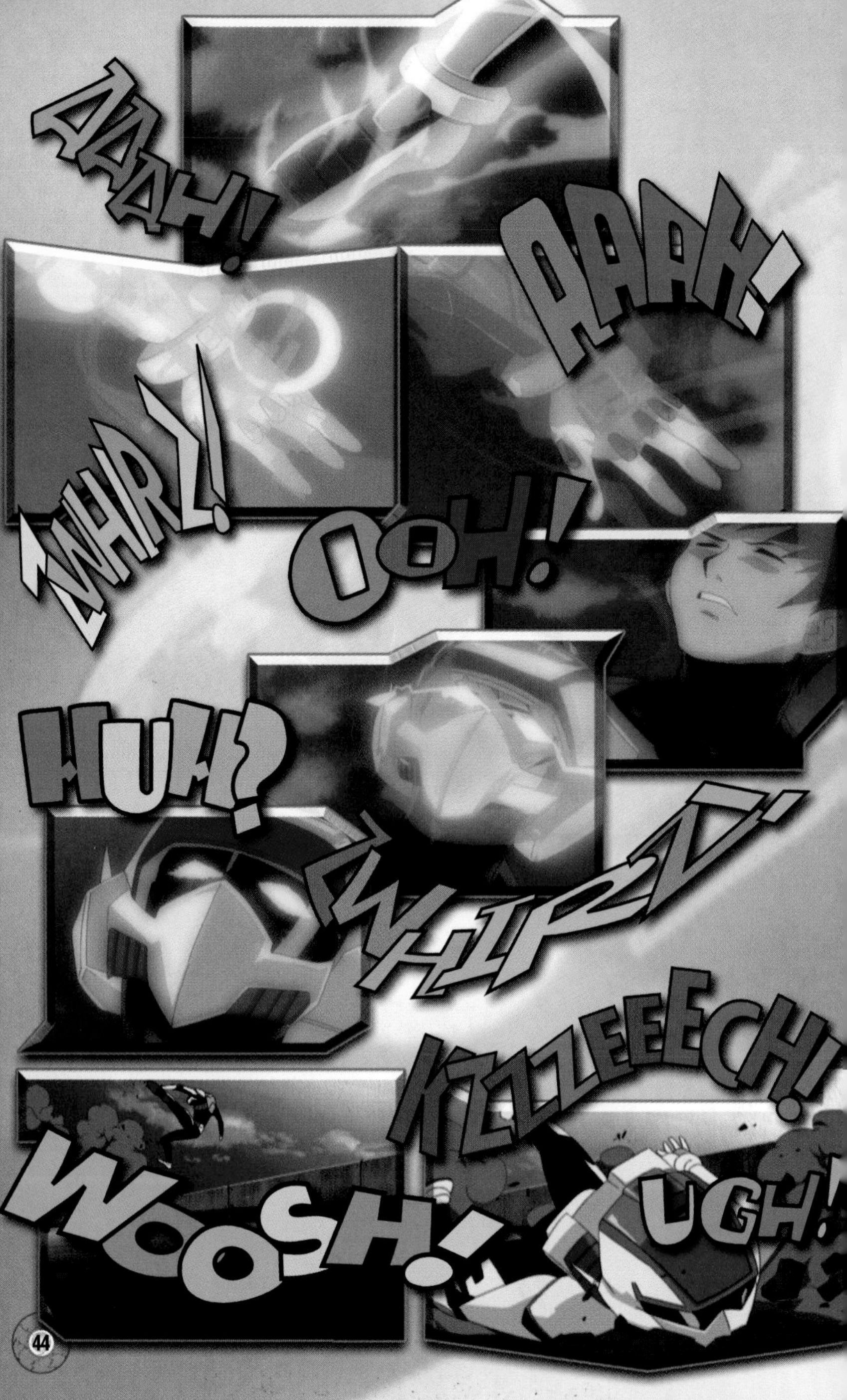
AAAH!
AAAH!
WHIRL!
OOOH!
HUH?
WHIRL
KZZZEEECH!
WOOSH!
UGH!

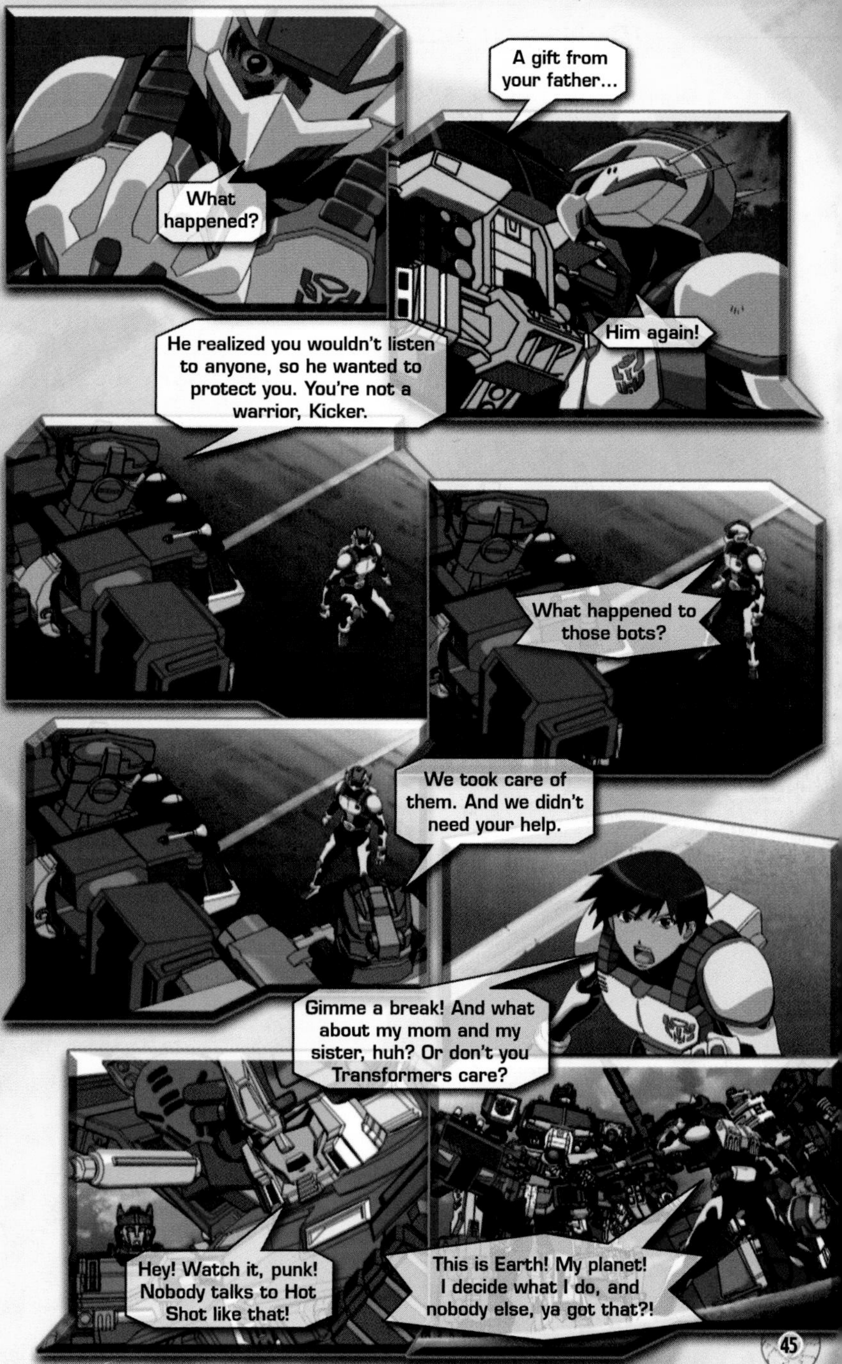
What happened?
A gift from your father...
Him again!
He realized you wouldn't listen to anyone, so he wanted to protect you. You're not a warrior, Kicker.
What happened to those bots?
We took care of them. And we didn't need your help.
Gimme a break! And what about my mom and my sister, huh? Or don't you Transformers care?
Hey! Watch it, punk! Nobody talks to Hot Shot like that!
This is Earth! My planet! I decide what I do, and nobody else, ya got that?!

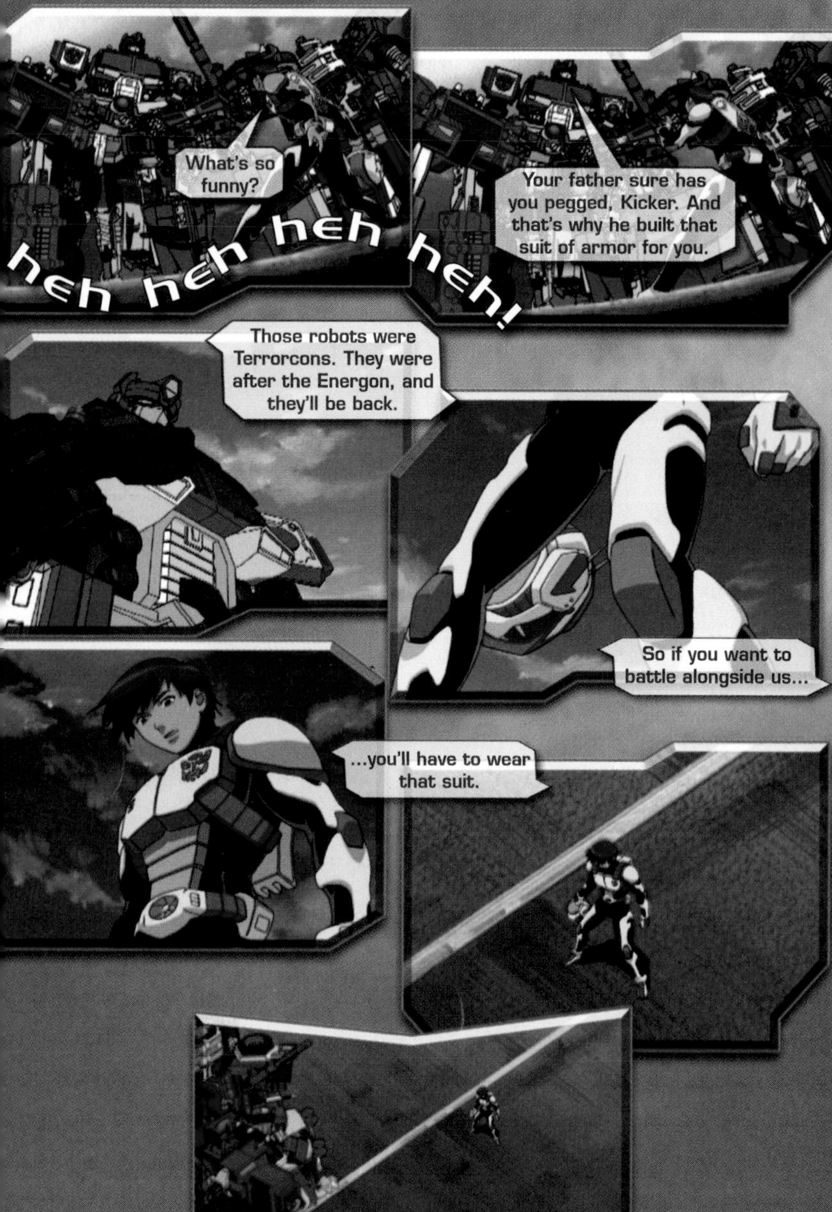
What's so funny?
heh heh heh heh!
Your father sure has you pegged, Kicker. And that's why he built that suit of armor for you.
Those robots were Terrorcons. They were after the Energon, and they'll be back.
So if you want to battle alongside us...
...you'll have to wear that suit.

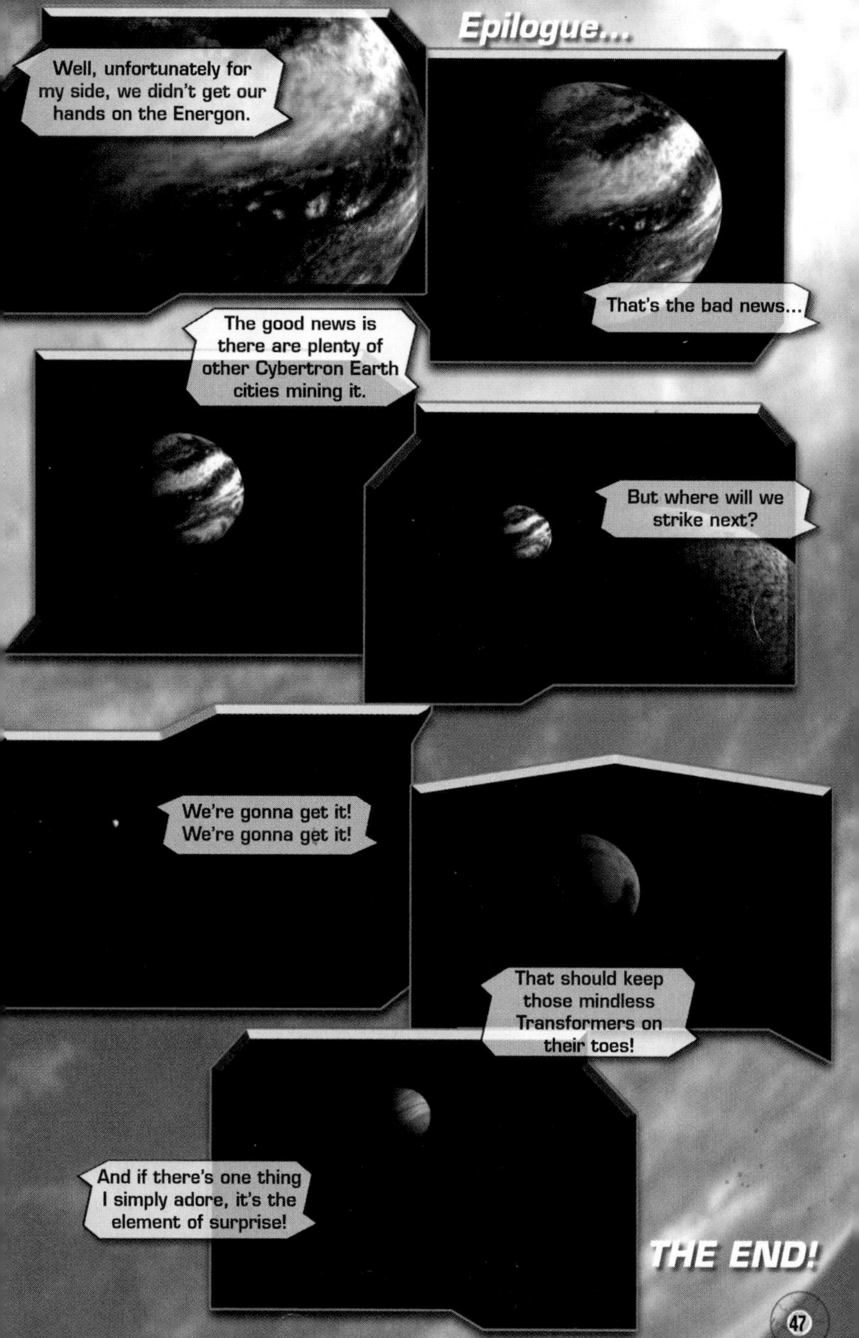
Epilogue...
Well, unfortunately for my side, we didn't get our hands on the Energon.
That's the bad news...
The good news is there are plenty of other Cybertron Earth cities mining it.
But where will we strike next?
We're gonna get it! We're gonna get it!
That should keep those mindless Transformers on their toes!
And if there's one thing I simply adore, it's the element of surprise!
THE END!

TRANSFORMERS ENERGON™ BRAND

ENERGON STARS

ENGLISH ADAPTATION: TERRY KLASSEN

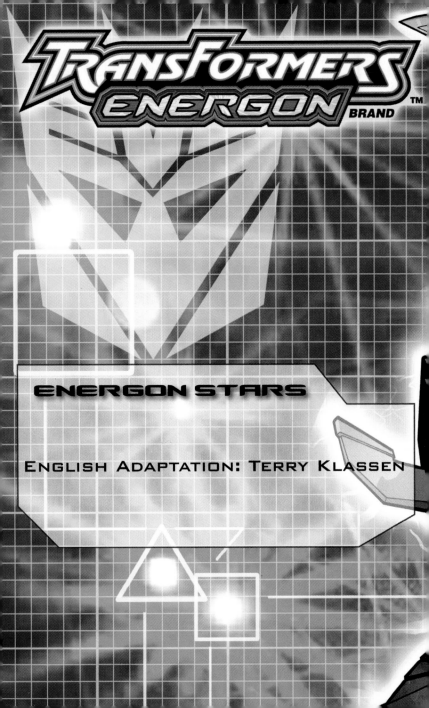

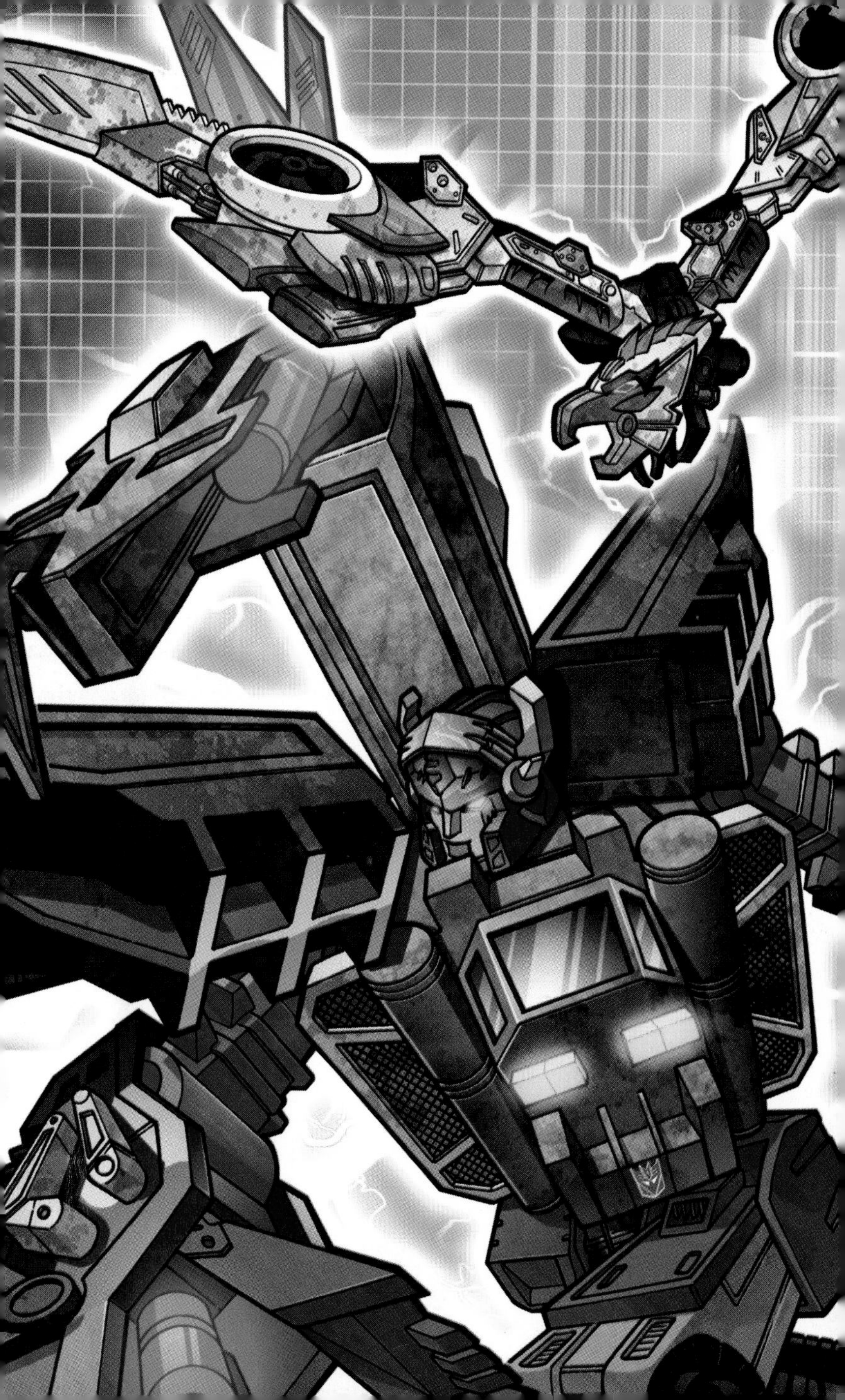

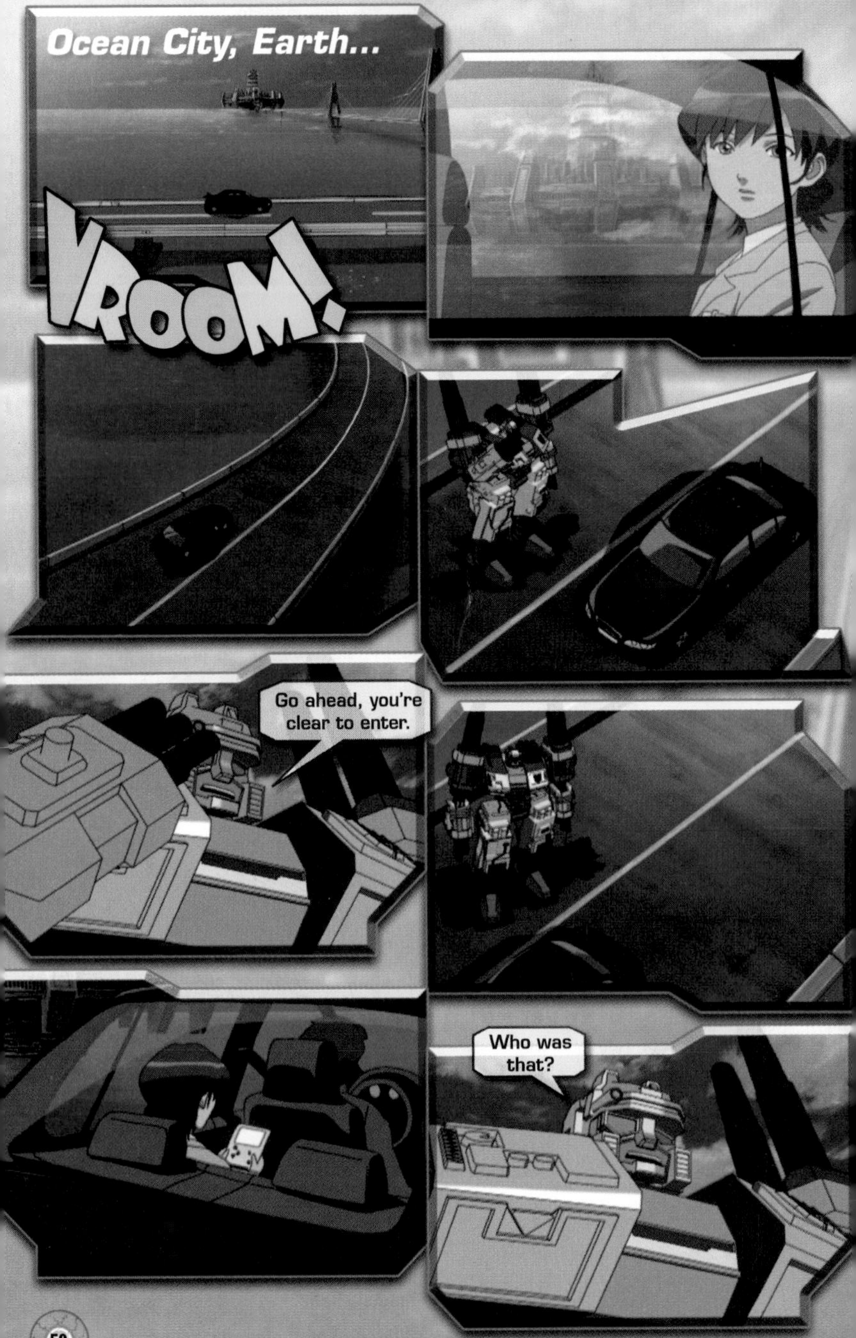
Ocean City, Earth...
VROOM!
Go ahead, you're clear to enter.
Who was that?

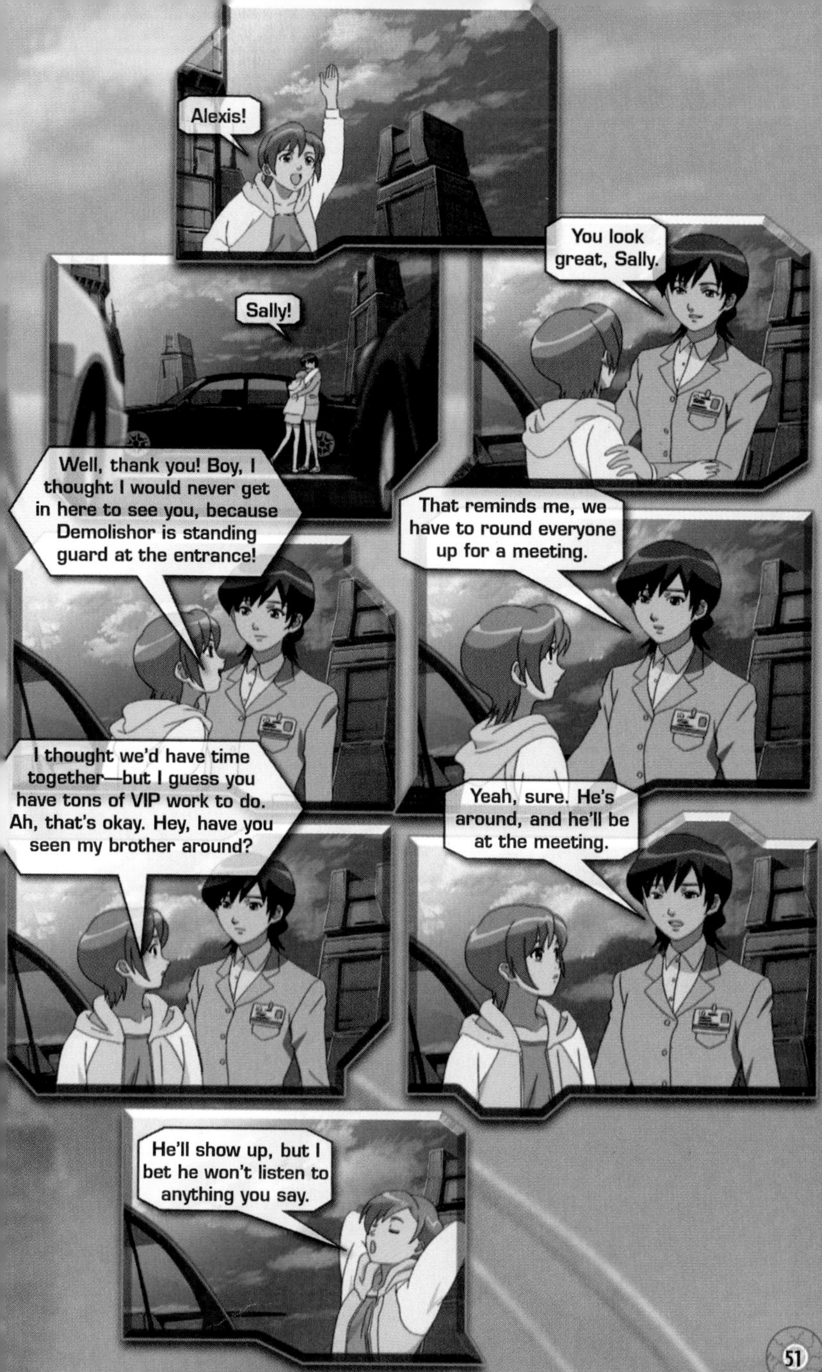
Alexis!
Sally!
You look great, Sally.
Well, thank you! Boy, I thought I would never get in here to see you, because Demolishor is standing guard at the entrance!
That reminds me, we have to round everyone up for a meeting.
I thought we'd have time together—but I guess you have tons of VIP work to do. Ah, that's okay. Hey, have you seen my brother around?
Yeah, sure. He's around, and he'll be at the meeting.
He'll show up, but I bet he won't listen to anything you say.

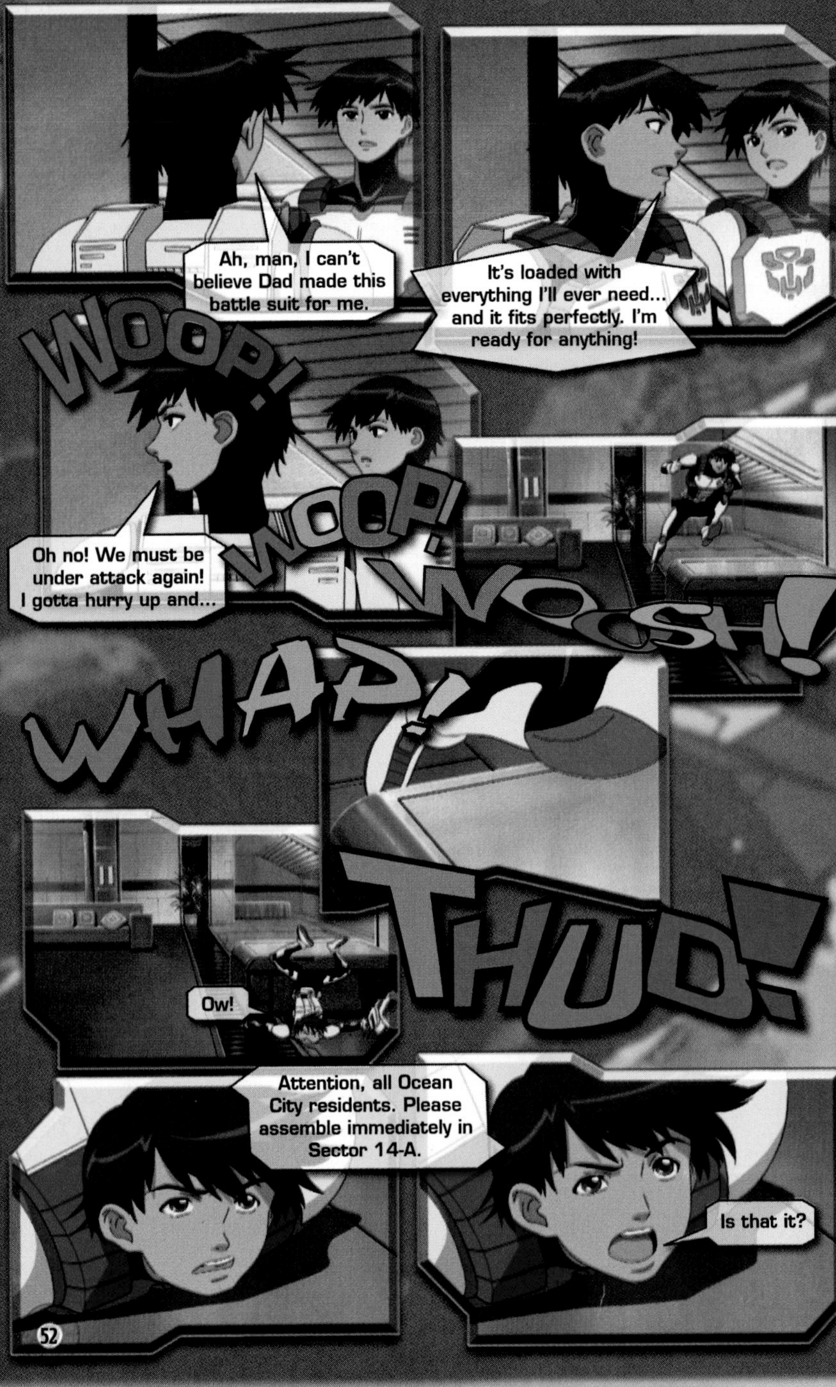

Ah, man, I can't believe Dad made this battle suit for me.
It's loaded with everything I'll ever need... and it fits perfectly. I'm ready for anything!
WOOP!
WOOP!
Oh no! We must be under attack again! I gotta hurry up and...
WOOSH!
WHAP!
THUD!
Ow!
Attention, all Ocean City residents. Please assemble immediately in Sector 14-A.
Is that it?

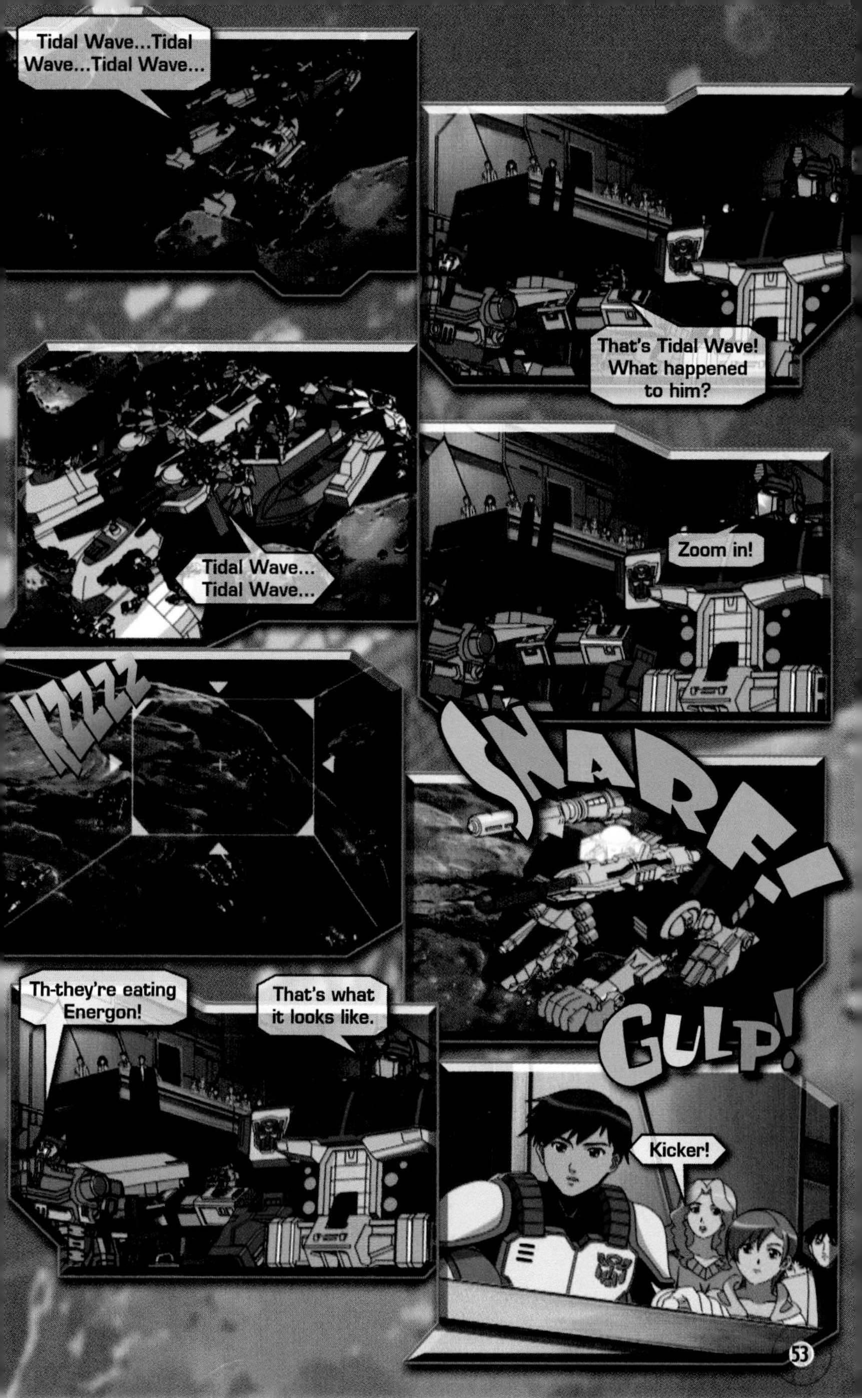

Tidal Wave...Tidal Wave...Tidal Wave...
That's Tidal Wave! What happened to him?
Tidal Wave... Tidal Wave...
Zoom in!
VZZZZ
SNARF!!
Th-they're eating Energon!
That's what it looks like.
GULP!
Kicker!

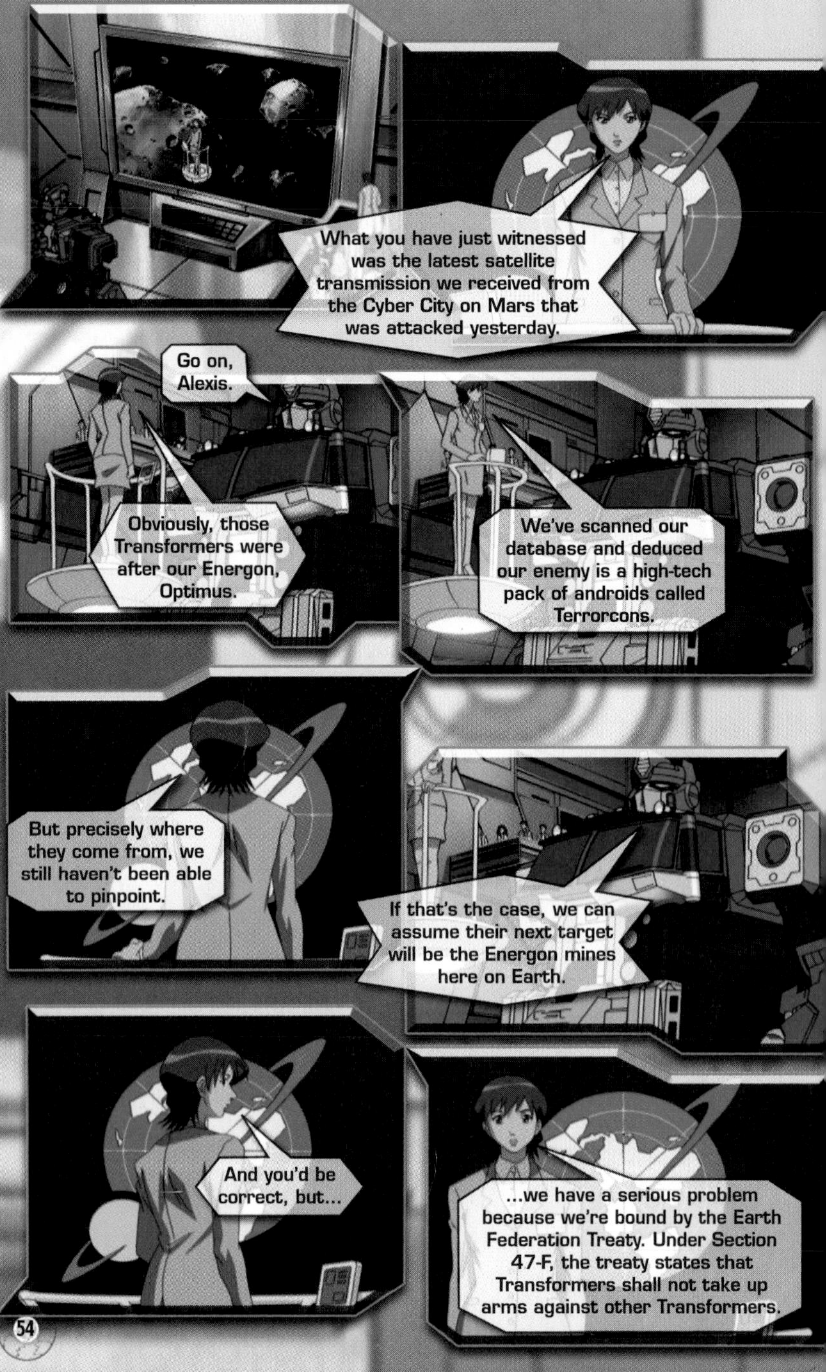
What you have just witnessed was the latest satellite transmission we received from the Cyber City on Mars that was attacked yesterday.
Go on, Alexis.
Obviously, those Transformers were after our Energon, Optimus.
We've scanned our database and deduced our enemy is a high-tech pack of androids called Terrorcons.
But precisely where they come from, we still haven't been able to pinpoint.
If that's the case, we can assume their next target will be the Energon mines here on Earth.
And you'd be correct, but...
...we have a serious problem because we're bound by the Earth Federation Treaty. Under Section 47-F, the treaty states that Transformers shall not take up arms against other Transformers.

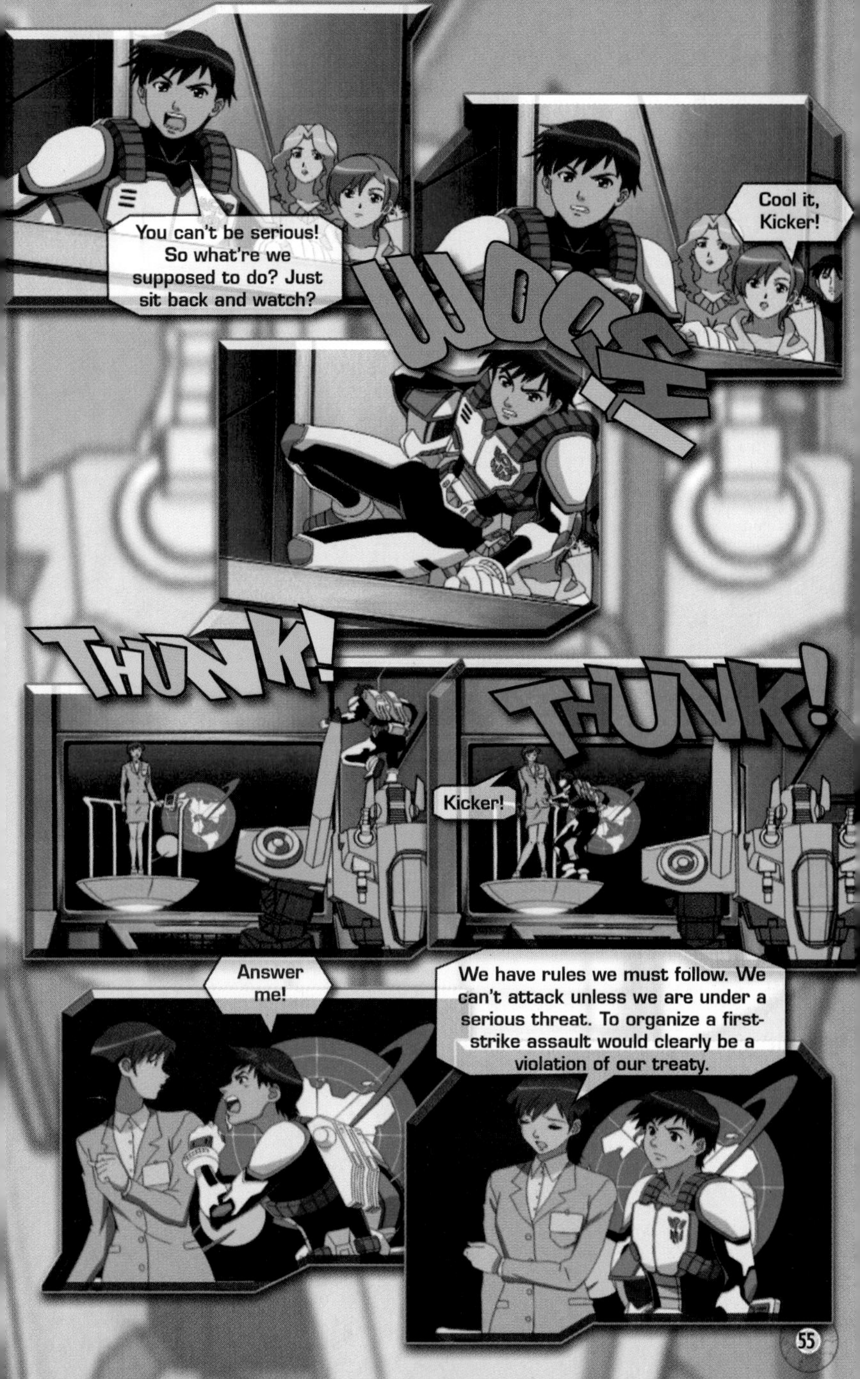

You can't be serious! So what're we supposed to do? Just sit back and watch?
Cool it, Kicker!
WOOSH
THUNK!
THUNK!
Kicker!
Answer me!
We have rules we must follow. We can't attack unless we are under a serious threat. To organize a first-strike assault would clearly be a violation of our treaty.

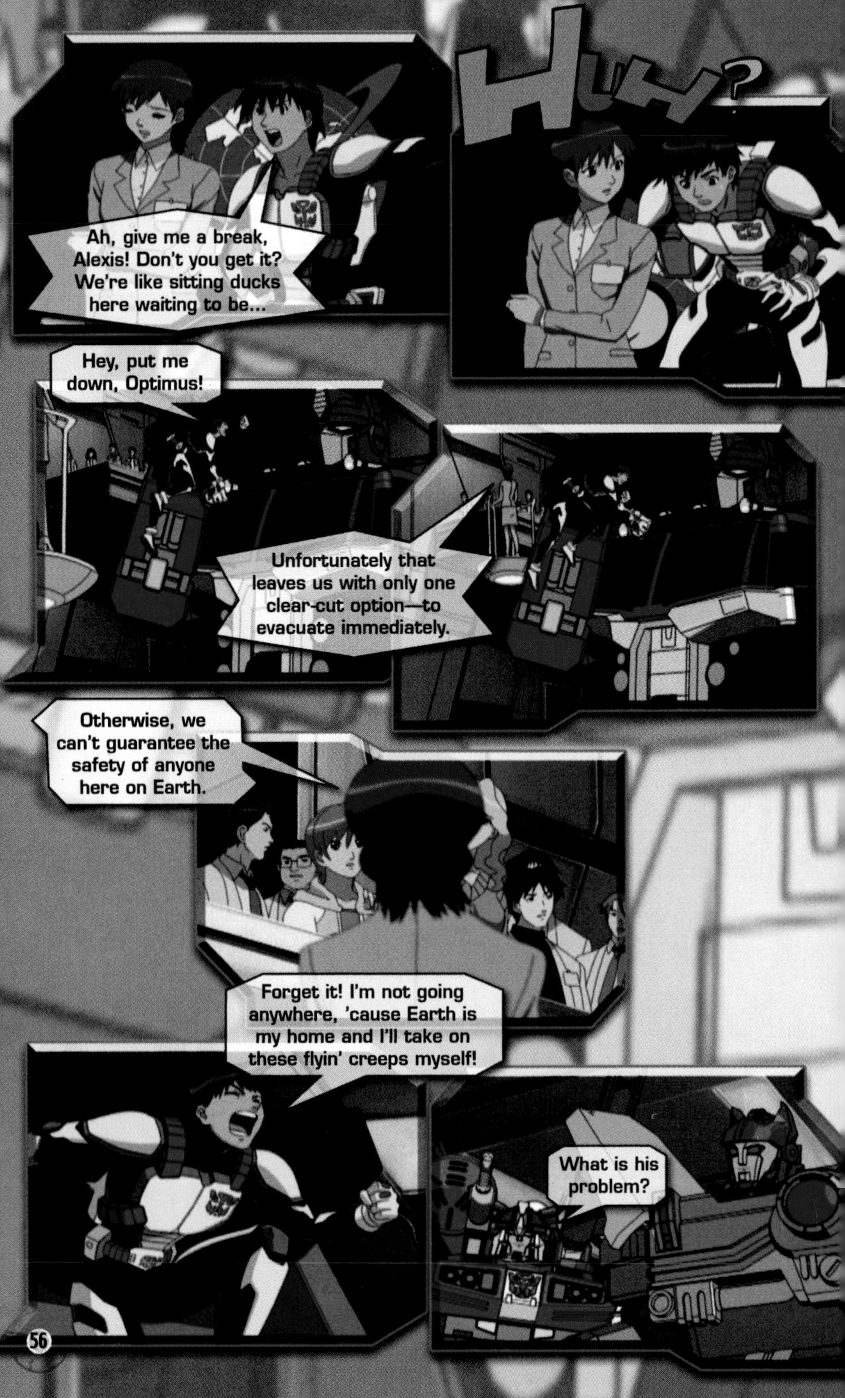
Ah, give me a break, Alexis! Don't you get it? We're like sitting ducks here waiting to be...
HUH?
Hey, put me down, Optimus!
Unfortunately that leaves us with only one clear-cut option—to evacuate immediately.
Otherwise, we can't guarantee the safety of anyone here on Earth.
Forget it! I'm not going anywhere, 'cause Earth is my home and I'll take on these flyin' creeps myself!
What is his problem?

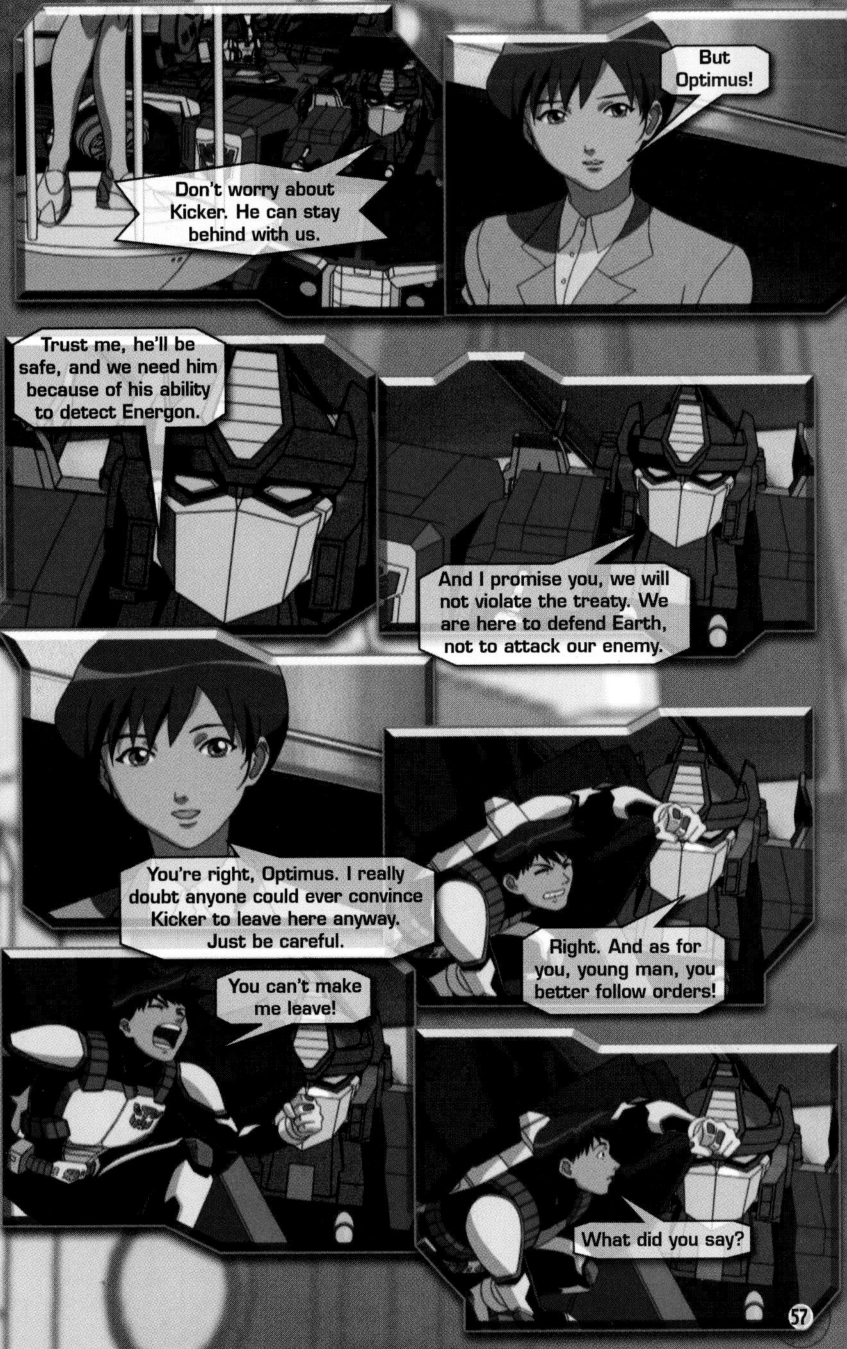
Don't worry about Kicker. He can stay behind with us.
But Optimus!
Trust me, he'll be safe, and we need him because of his ability to detect Energon.
And I promise you, we will not violate the treaty. We are here to defend Earth, not to attack our enemy.
You're right, Optimus. I really doubt anyone could ever convince Kicker to leave here anyway. Just be careful.
Right. And as for you, young man, you better follow orders!
You can't make me leave!
What did you say?

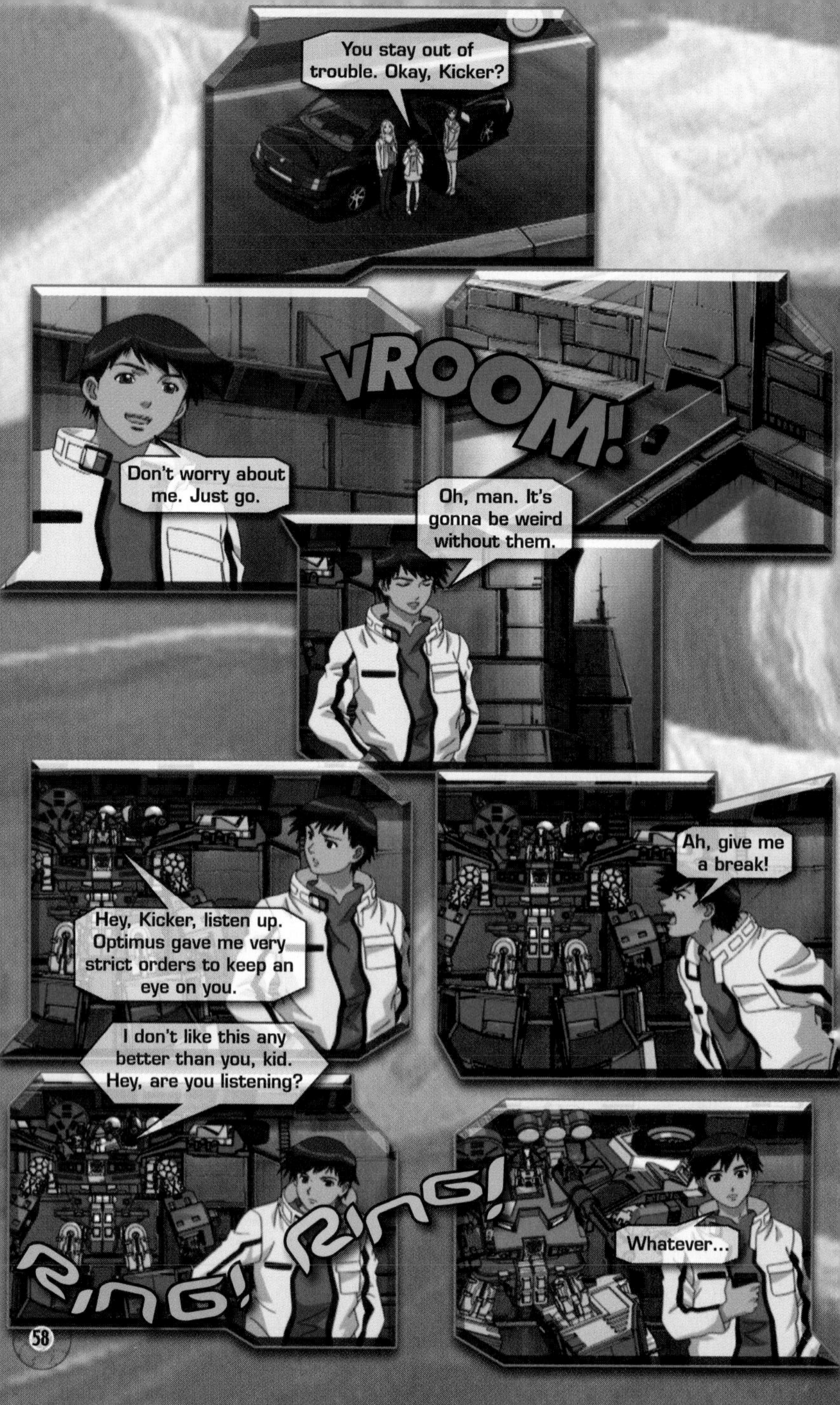
You stay out of trouble. Okay, Kicker?
Don't worry about me. Just go.
VROOM!
Oh, man. It's gonna be weird without them.
Hey, Kicker, listen up. Optimus gave me very strict orders to keep an eye on you.
Ah, give me a break!
I don't like this any better than you, kid. Hey, are you listening?
RING! RING!
Whatever...

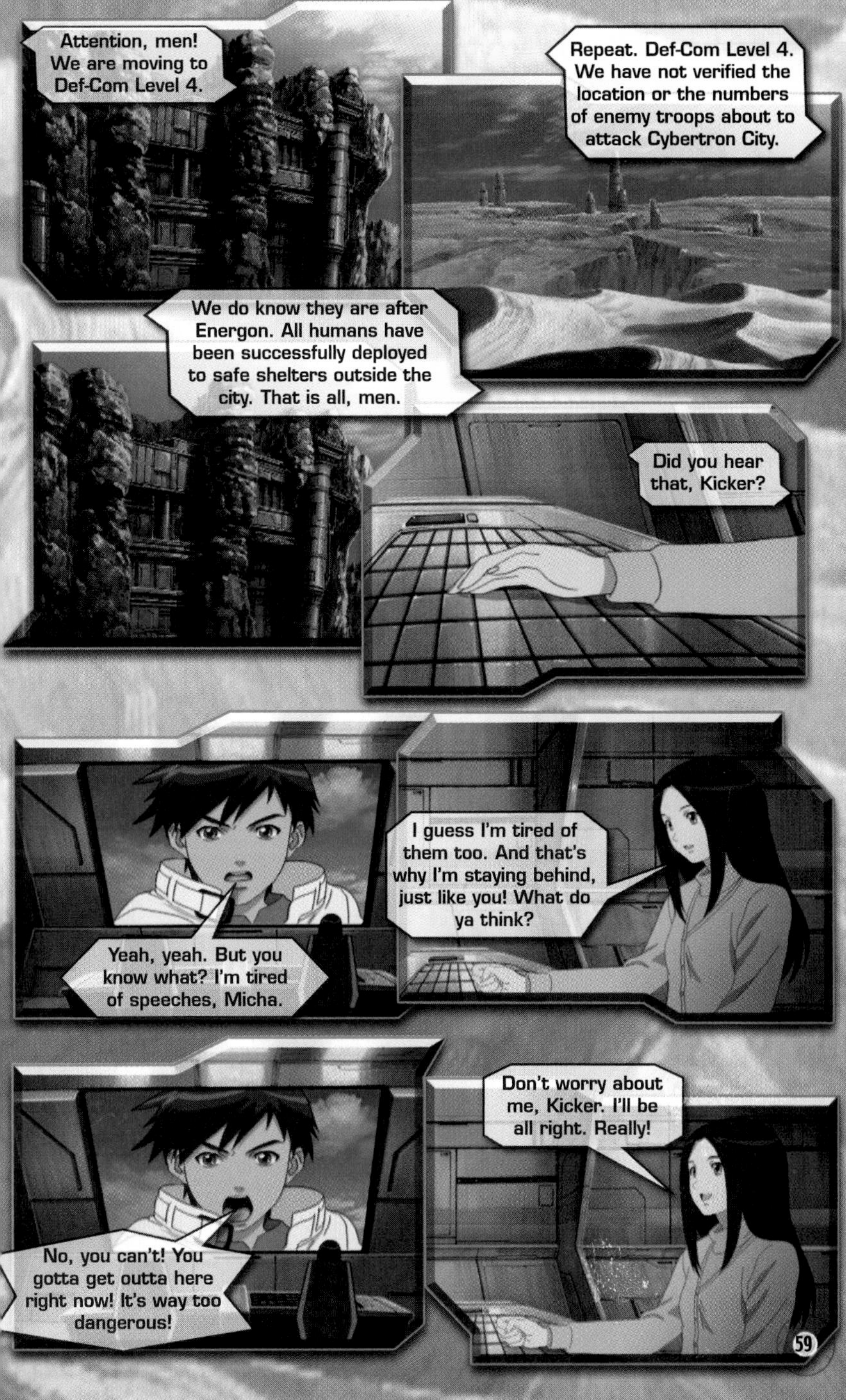
Attention, men! We are moving to Def-Com Level 4.
Repeat. Def-Com Level 4. We have not verified the location or the numbers of enemy troops about to attack Cybertron City.
We do know they are after Energon. All humans have been successfully deployed to safe shelters outside the city. That is all, men.
Did you hear that, Kicker?
Yeah, yeah. But you know what? I'm tired of speeches, Micha.
I guess I'm tired of them too. And that's why I'm staying behind, just like you! What do ya think?
No, you can't! You gotta get outta here right now! It's way too dangerous!
Don't worry about me, Kicker. I'll be all right. Really!

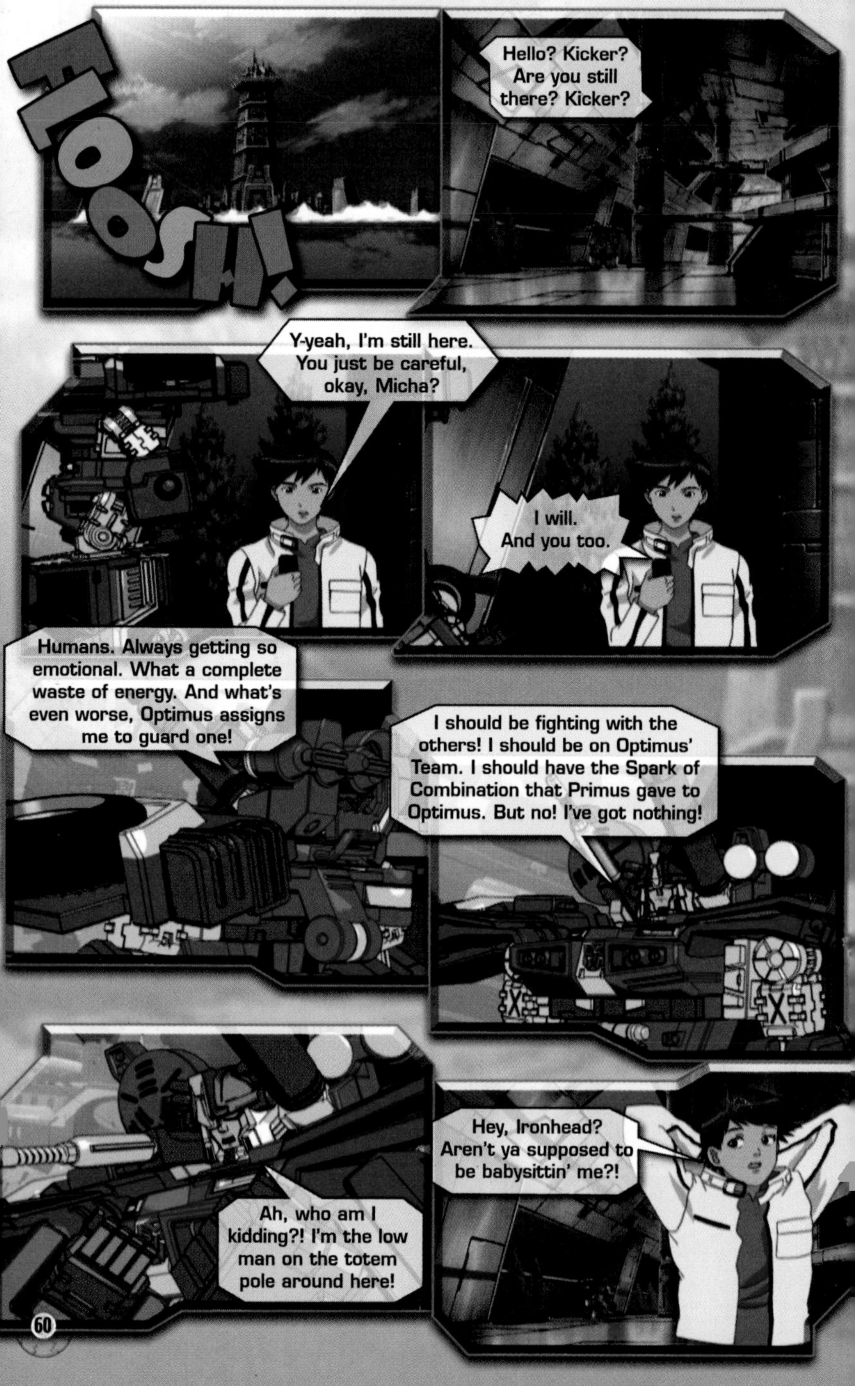
FLOOSH!
Hello? Kicker? Are you still there? Kicker?
Y-yeah, I'm still here. You just be careful, okay, Micha?
I will. And you too.
Humans. Always getting so emotional. What a complete waste of energy. And what's even worse, Optimus assigns me to guard one!
I should be fighting with the others! I should be on Optimus' Team. I should have the Spark of Combination that Primus gave to Optimus. But no! I've got nothing!
Ah, who am I kidding?! I'm the low man on the totem pole around here!
Hey, Ironhead? Aren't ya supposed to be babysittin' me?!

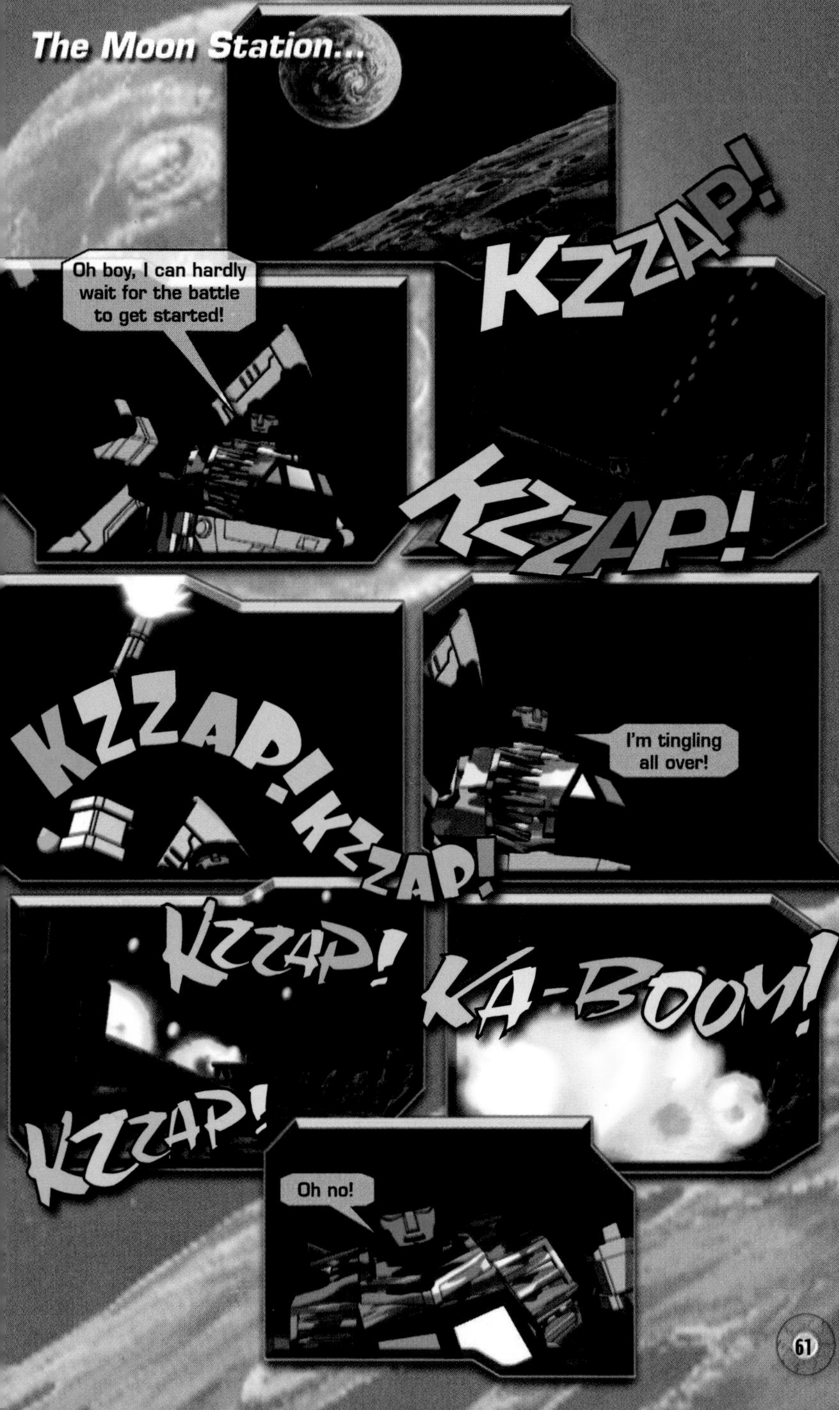
The Moon Station...
Oh boy, I can hardly wait for the battle to get started!
KZZAP!
KZZAP!
KZZAP!
KZZAP!
I'm tingling all over!
KZZAP!
KA-BOOM!
KZZAP!
Oh no!

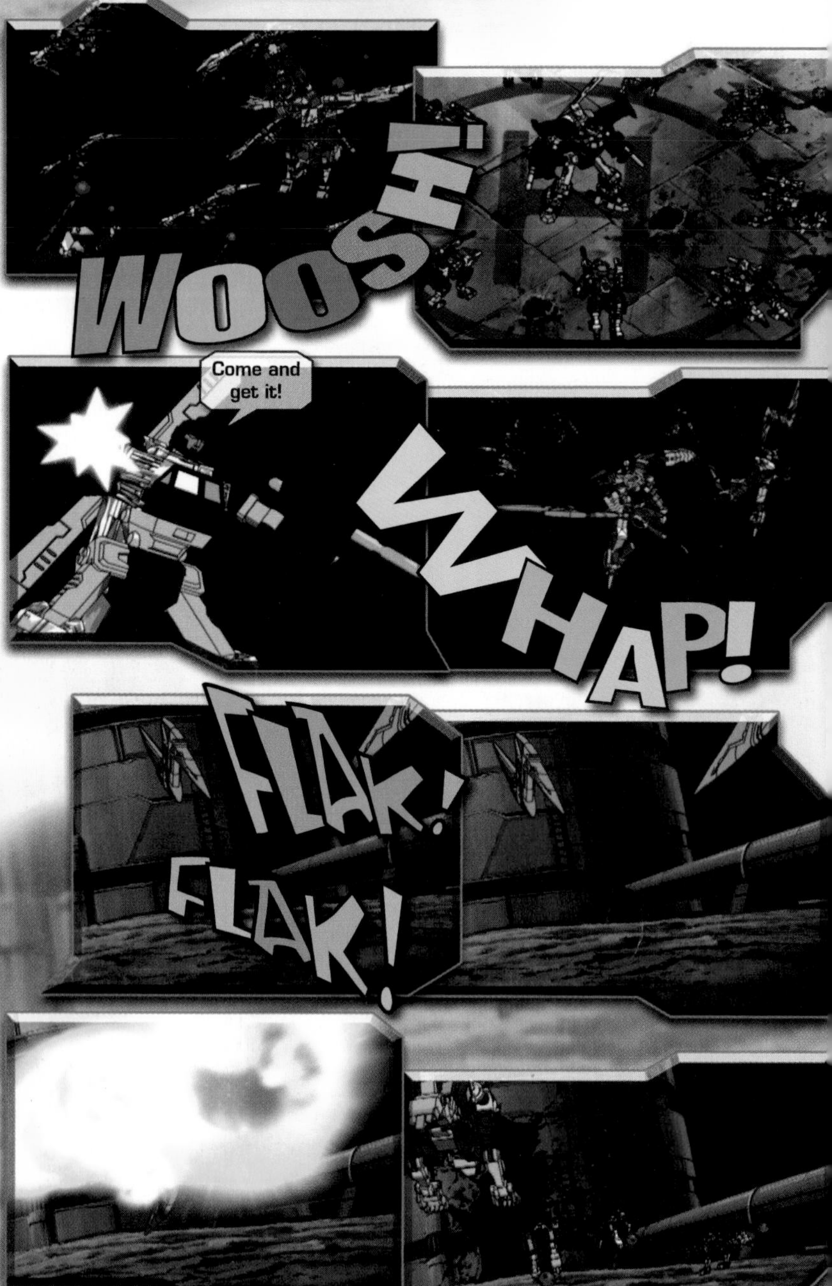
WOOSH!
Come and get it!
WHAP!
FLAK!
FLAK!

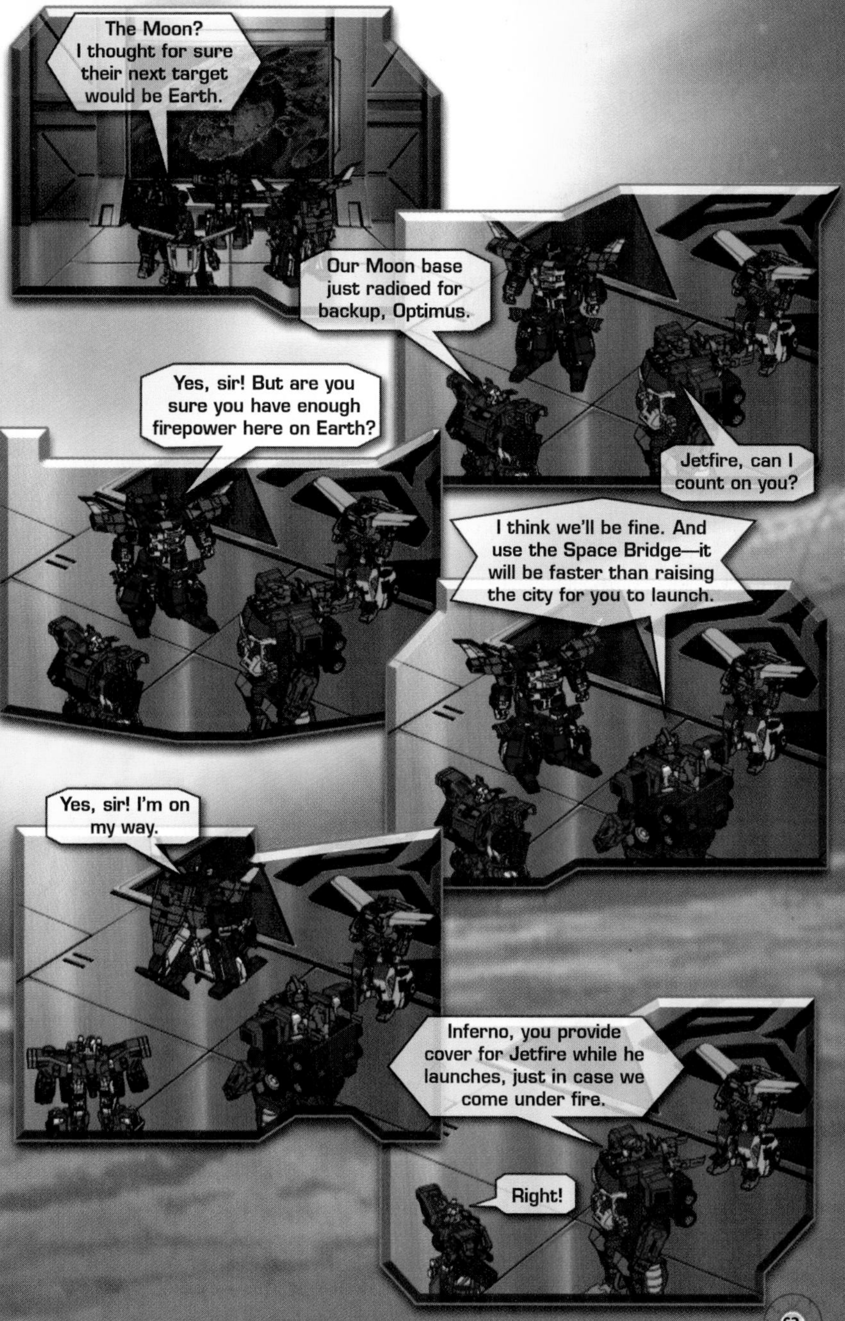
The Moon? I thought for sure their next target would be Earth.
Our Moon base just radioed for backup, Optimus.
Jetfire, can I count on you?
Yes, sir! But are you sure you have enough firepower here on Earth?
I think we'll be fine. And use the Space Bridge—it will be faster than raising the city for you to launch.
Yes, sir! I'm on my way.
Inferno, you provide cover for Jetfire while he launches, just in case we come under fire.
Right!

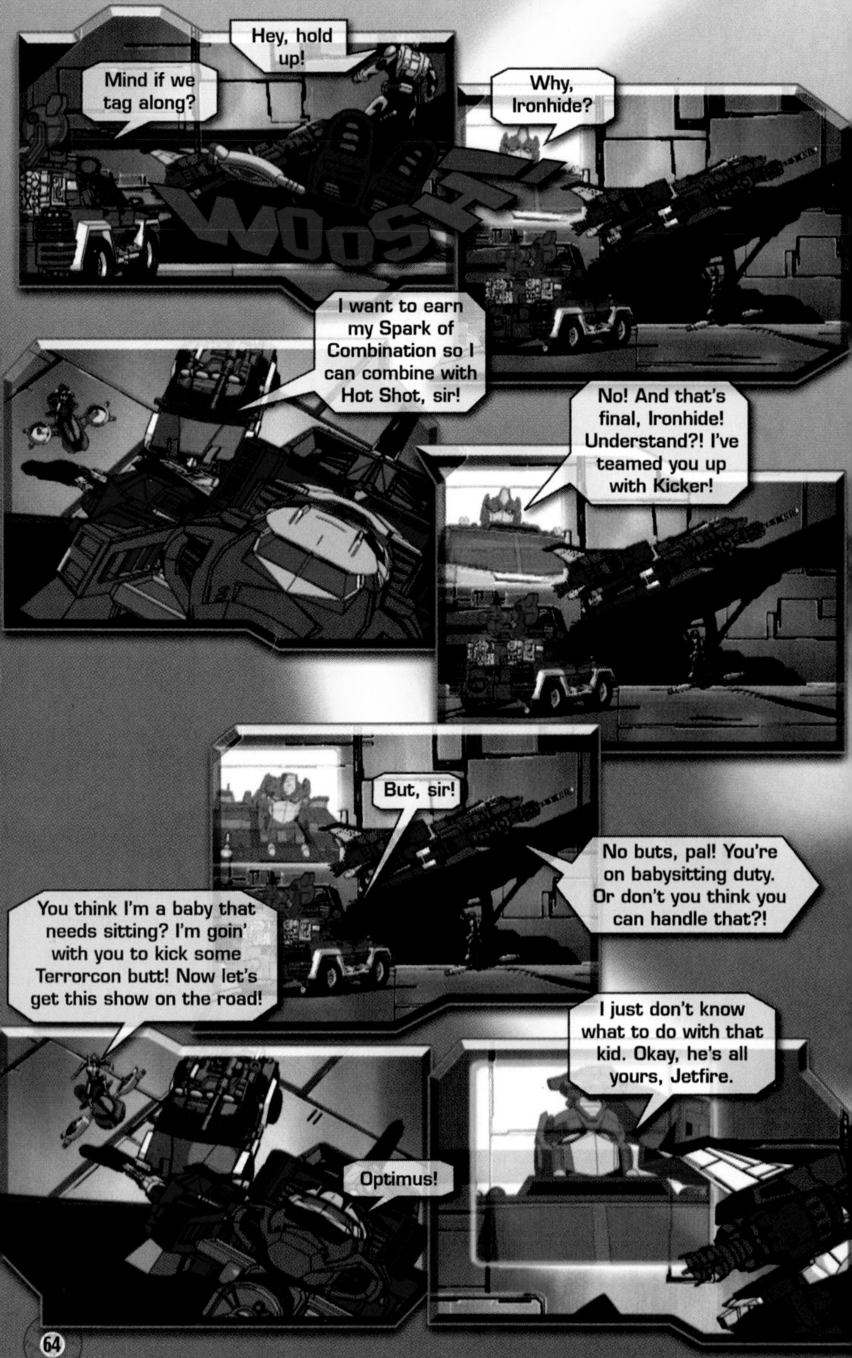
Hey, hold up!
Mind if we tag along?
WOOSH!
Why, Ironhide?
I want to earn my Spark of Combination so I can combine with Hot Shot, sir!
No! And that's final, Ironhide! Understand?! I've teamed you up with Kicker!
But, sir!
No buts, pal! You're on babysitting duty. Or don't you think you can handle that?!
You think I'm a baby that needs sitting? I'm goin' with you to kick some Terrorcon butt! Now let's get this show on the road!
I just don't know what to do with that kid. Okay, he's all yours, Jetfire.
Optimus!

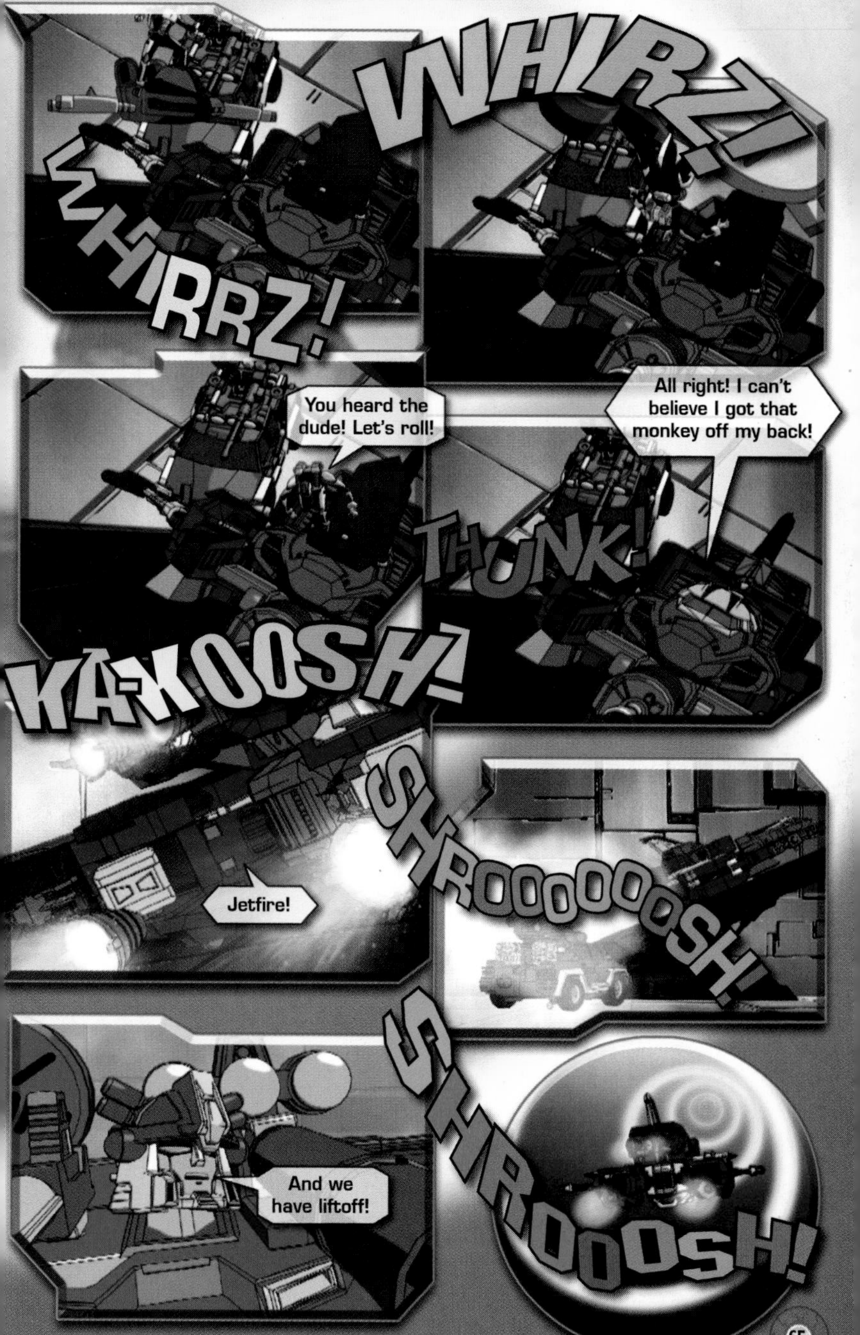
WHIRRRZ!
WHIRRZ!
You heard the dude! Let's roll!
All right! I can't believe I got that monkey off my back!
THUNK!
KA-KOOSH!
Jetfire!
SHROOOOOOOSH!
And we have liftoff!
SHROOOSH!

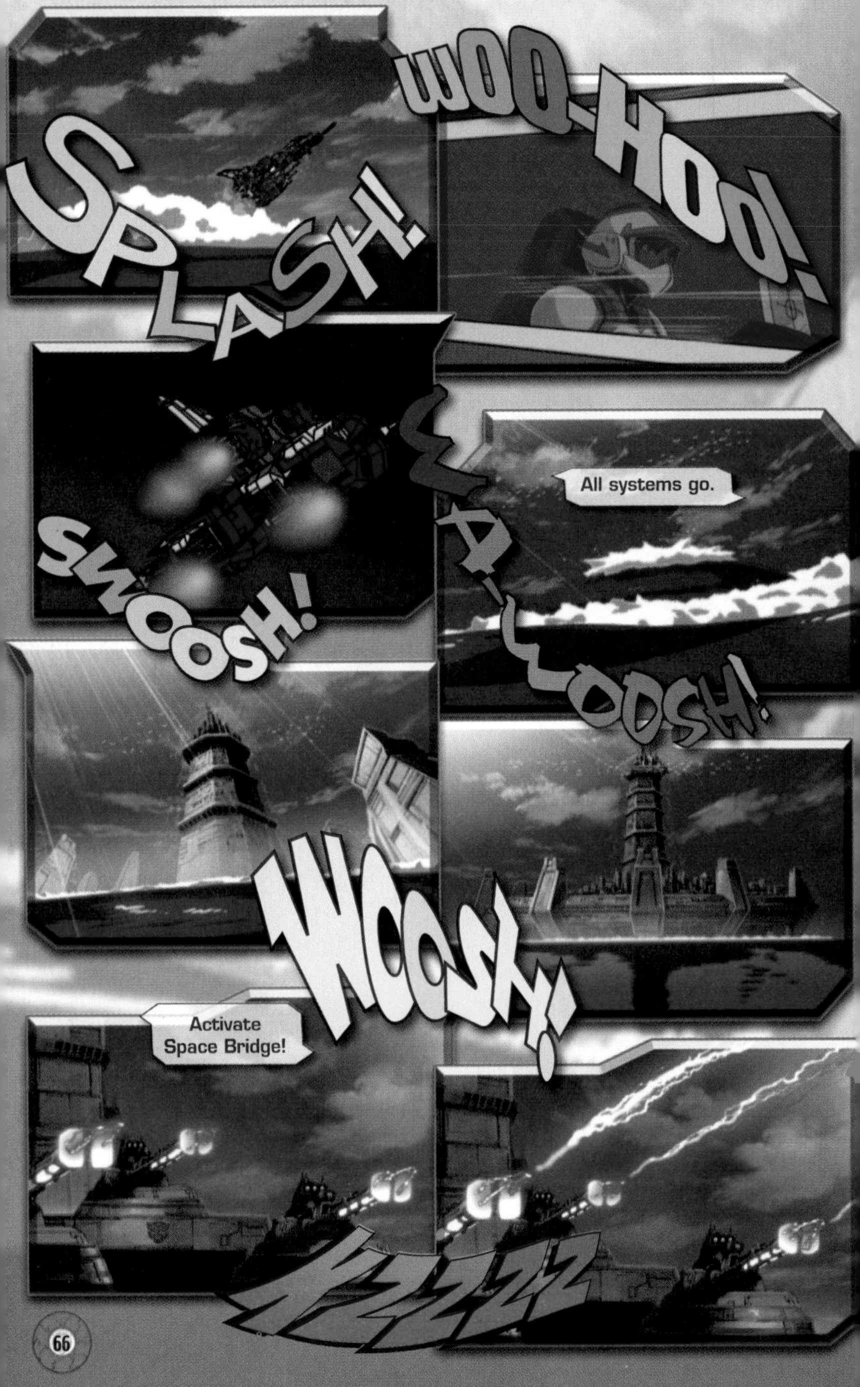
SPLASH!
WOO-HOO!
SWOOSH!
WA-WOOSH!
All systems go.
WHOOSH!
Activate Space Bridge!

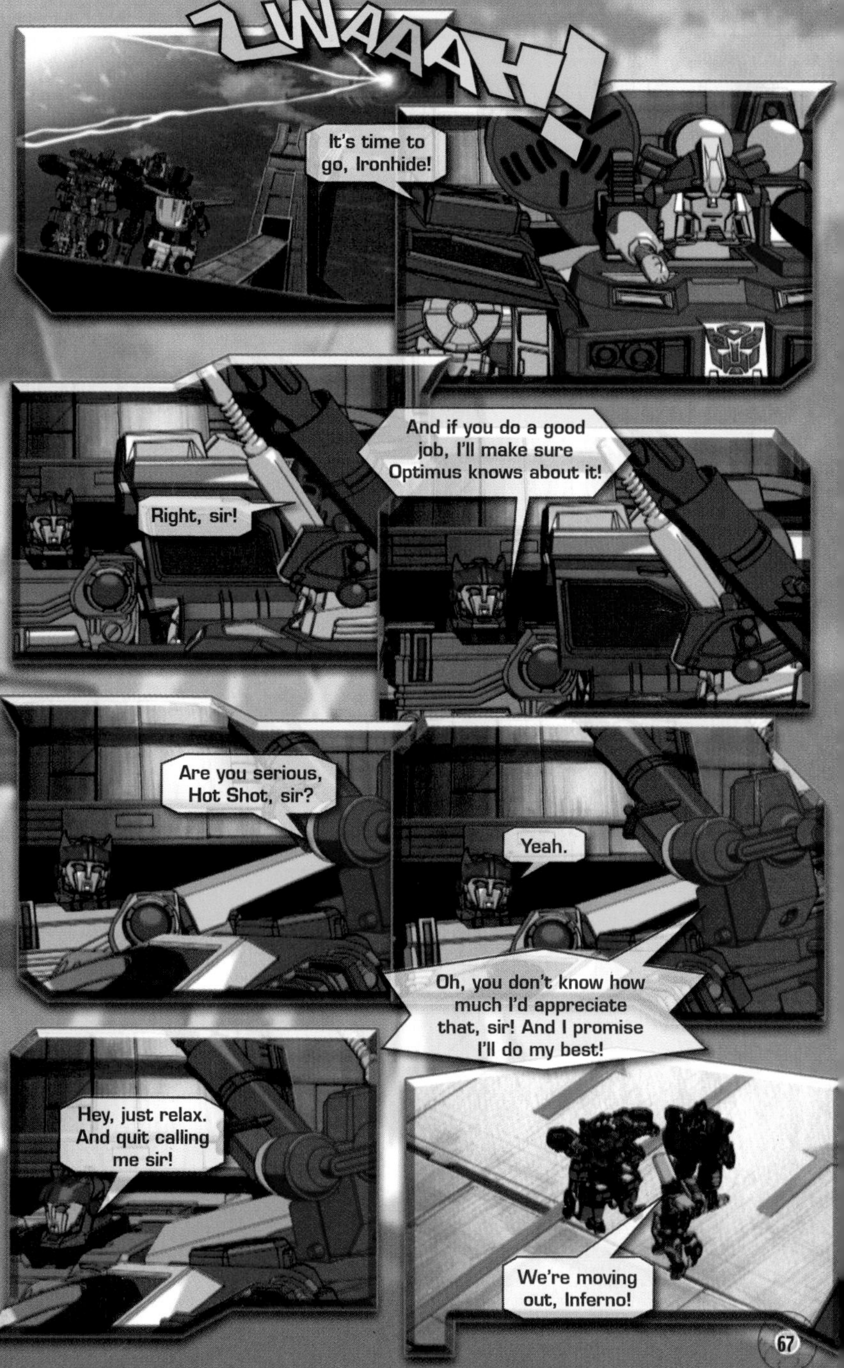
ZWAAAH!
It's time to go, Ironhide!
Right, sir!
And if you do a good job, I'll make sure Optimus knows about it!
Are you serious, Hot Shot, sir?
Yeah.
Oh, you don't know how much I'd appreciate that, sir! And I promise I'll do my best!
Hey, just relax. And quit calling me sir!
We're moving out, Inferno!

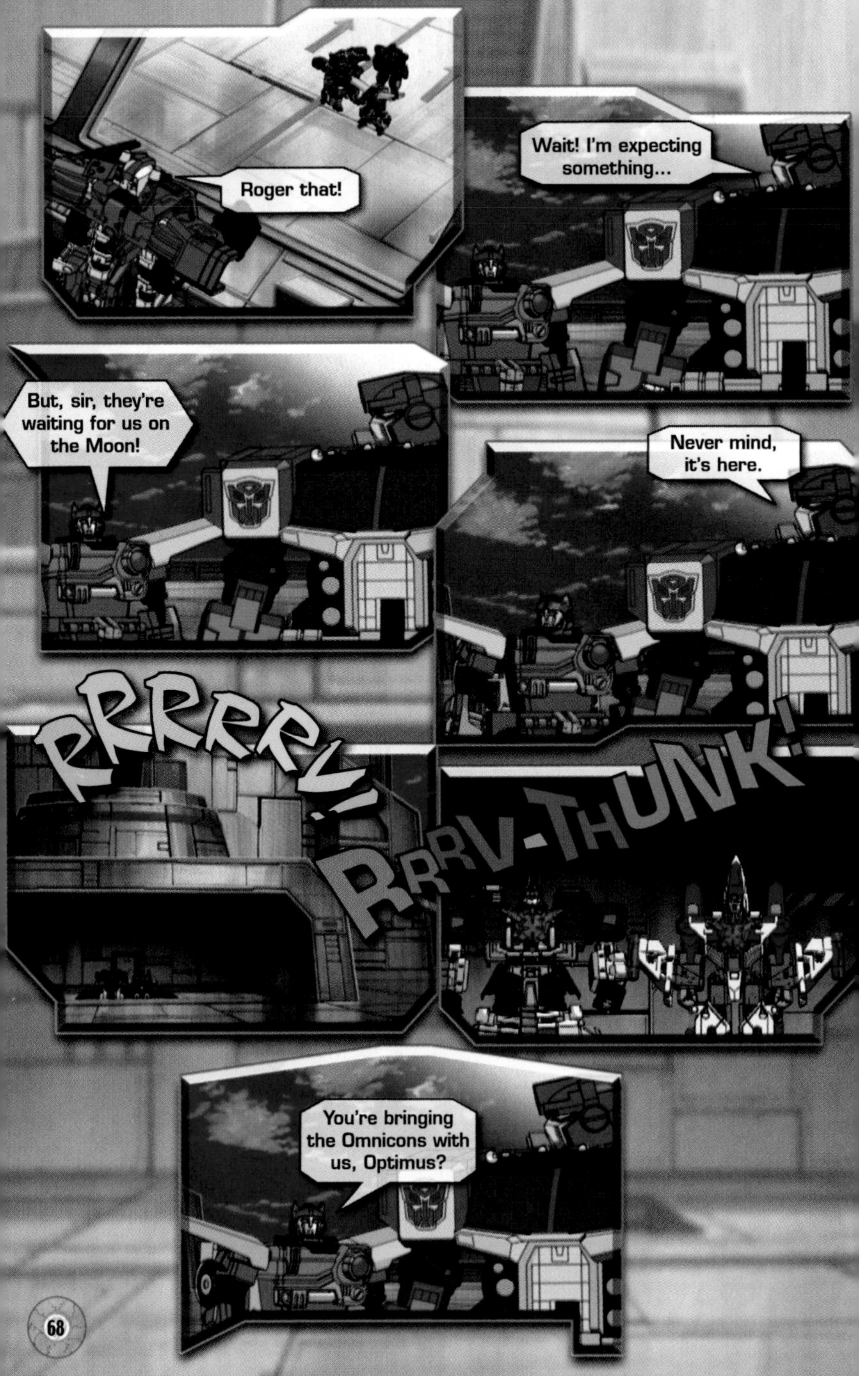
Roger that!
Wait! I'm expecting something...
But, sir, they're waiting for us on the Moon!
Never mind, it's here.
RRRRRV!
RRRRV-THUNK!
You're bringing the Omnicons with us, Optimus?

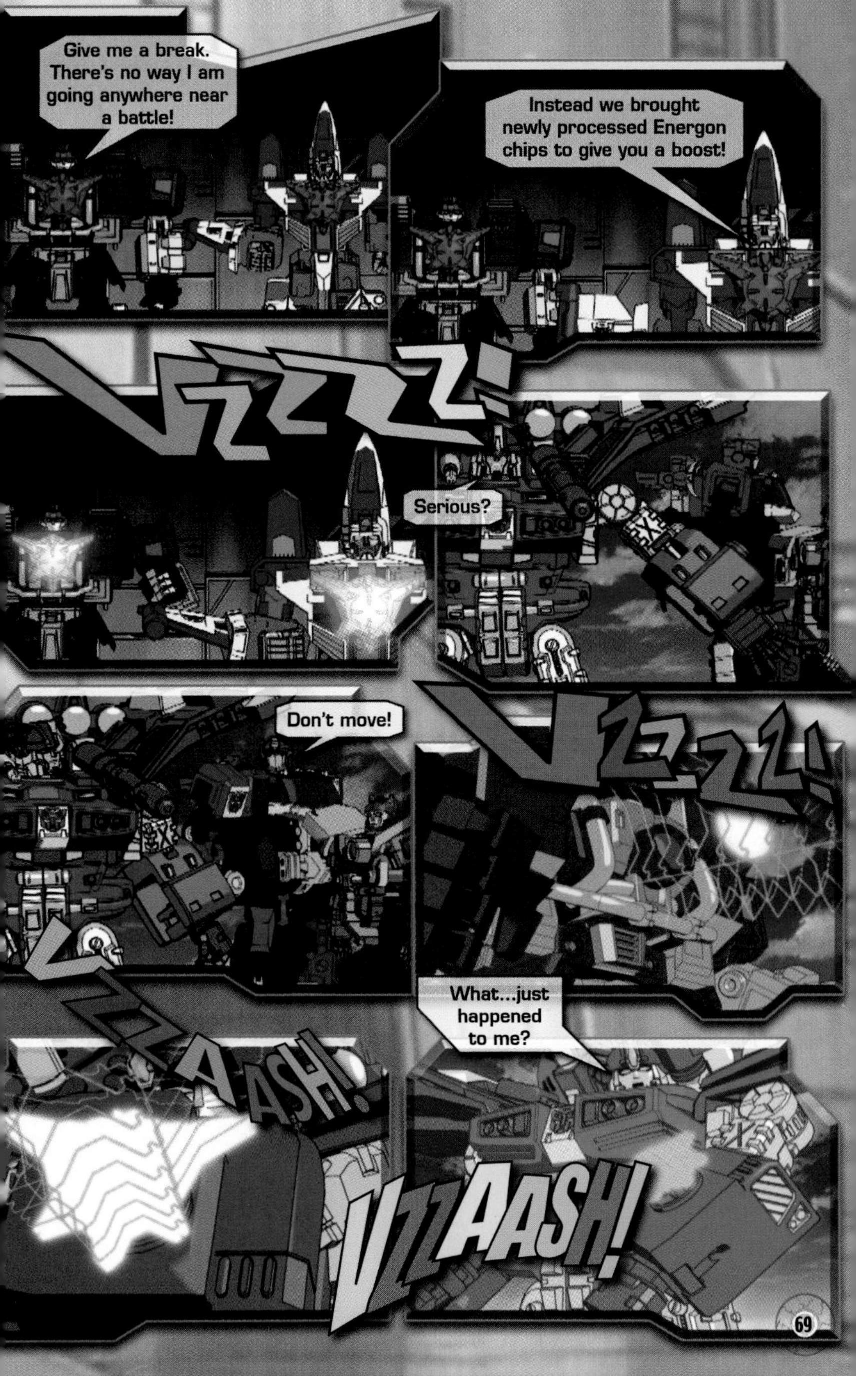
Give me a break. There's no way I am going anywhere near a battle!
Instead we brought newly processed Energon chips to give you a boost!
VZZZZ!
Serious?
Don't move!
VZZZZ!
VZZAASH!
What...just happened to me?
VZZAASH!

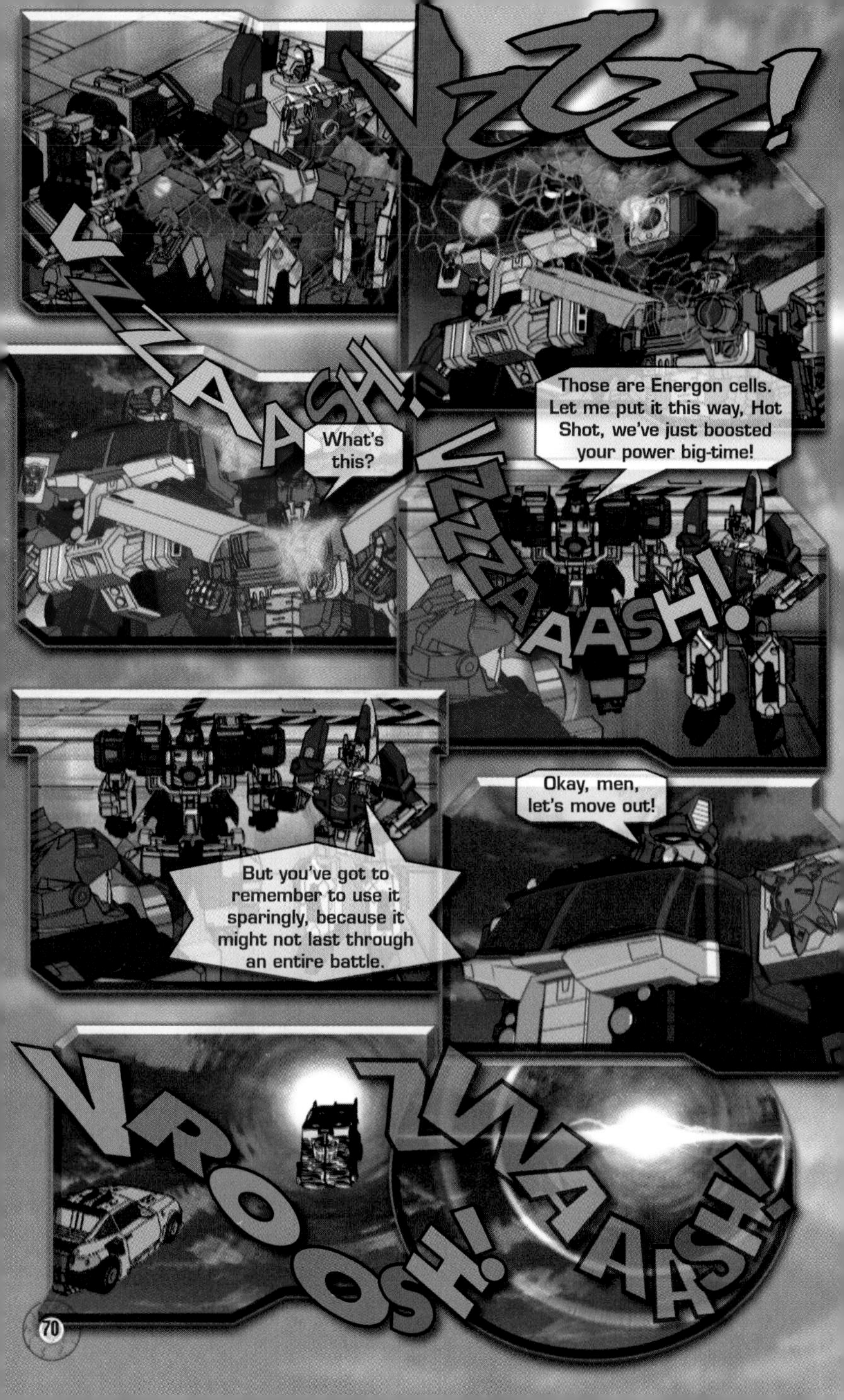
What's this?
Those are Energon cells. Let me put it this way, Hot Shot, we've just boosted your power big-time!
But you've got to remember to use it sparingly, because it might not last through an entire battle.
Okay, men, let's move out!
VROOOSH!

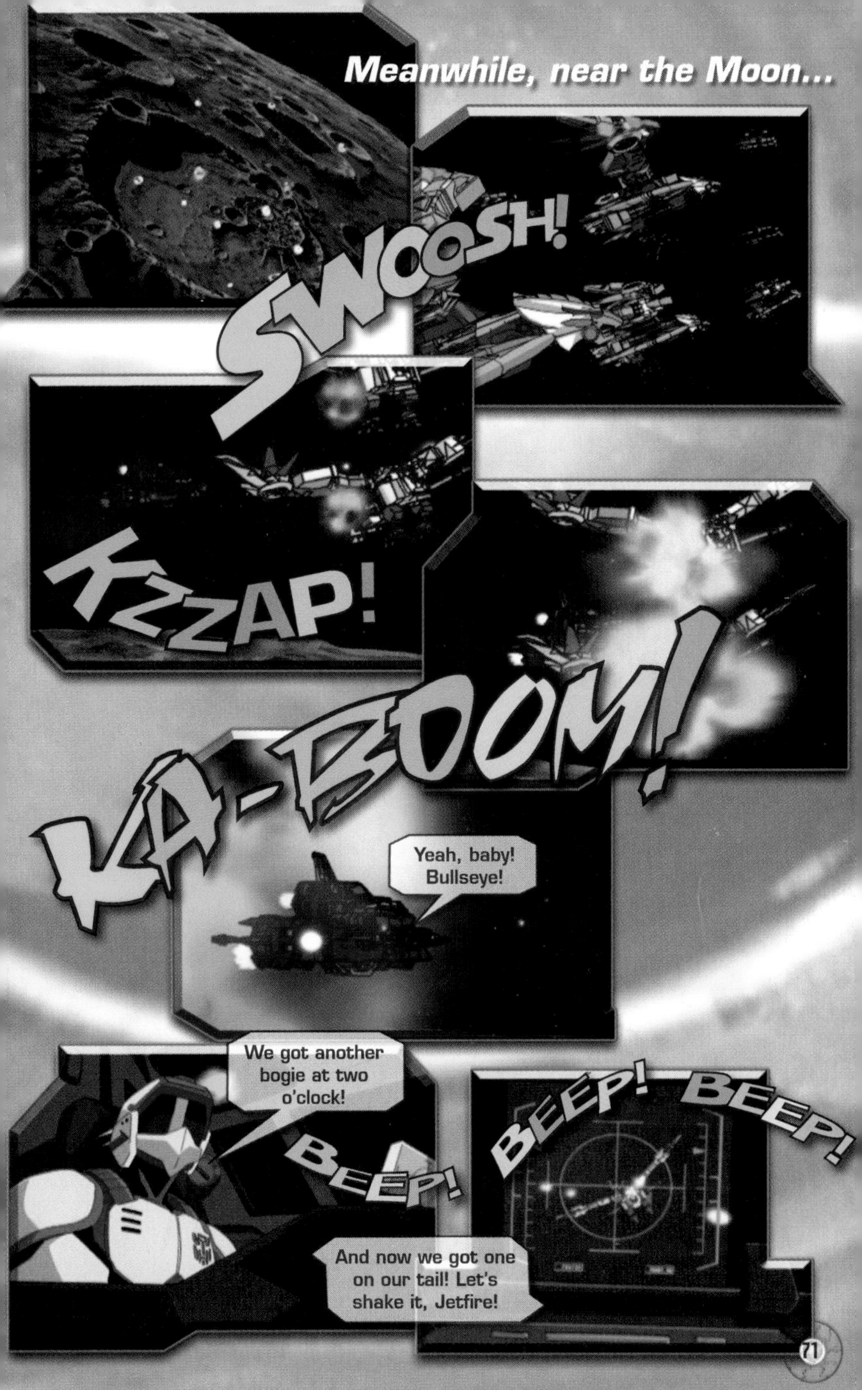
Meanwhile, near the Moon...
SWOOSH!
KZZAP!
KA-BOOM!
Yeah, baby! Bullseye!
We got another bogie at two o'clock!
BEEP!
BEEP!
BEEP!
And now we got one on our tail! Let's shake it, Jetfire!

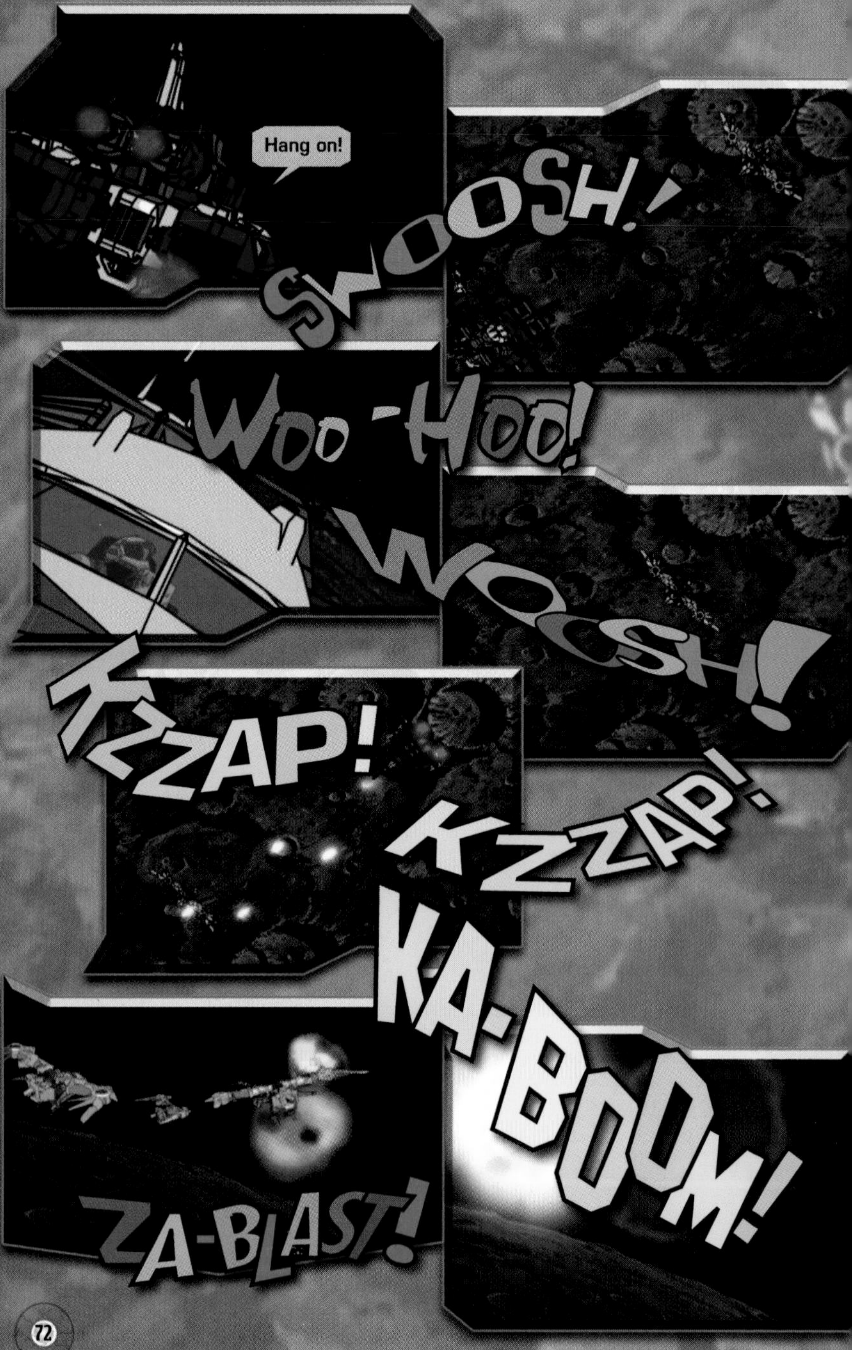
Hang on!
SWOOSH!
WOO-HOO!
WOOSH!
KZZAP!
KZZAP!
KA-BOOM!
ZA-BLAST!

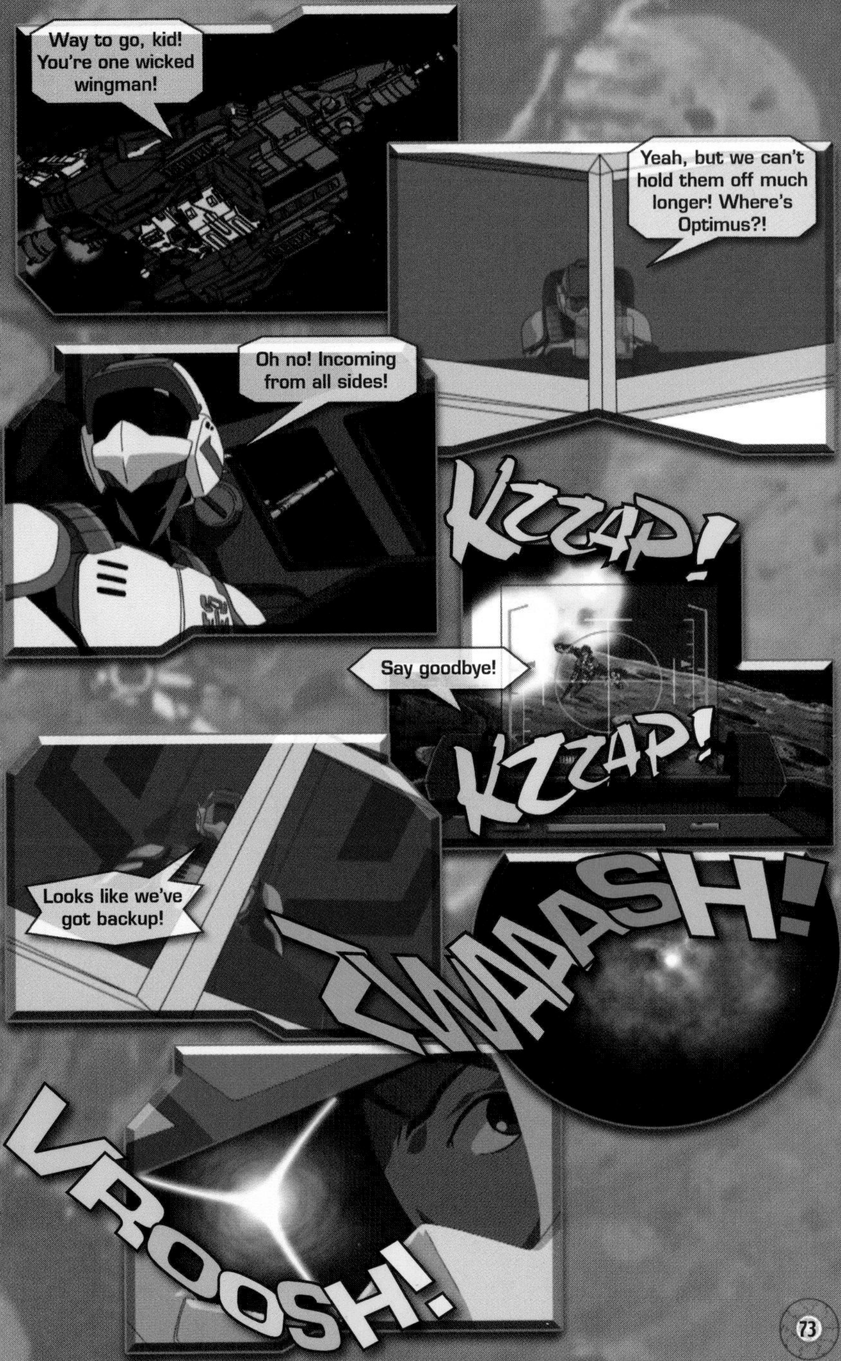

Way to go, kid! You're one wicked wingman!
Yeah, but we can't hold them off much longer! Where's Optimus?!
Oh no! Incoming from all sides!
KZZAP!
Say goodbye!
KZZAP!
Looks like we've got backup!
VWAASH!
VROOSH!

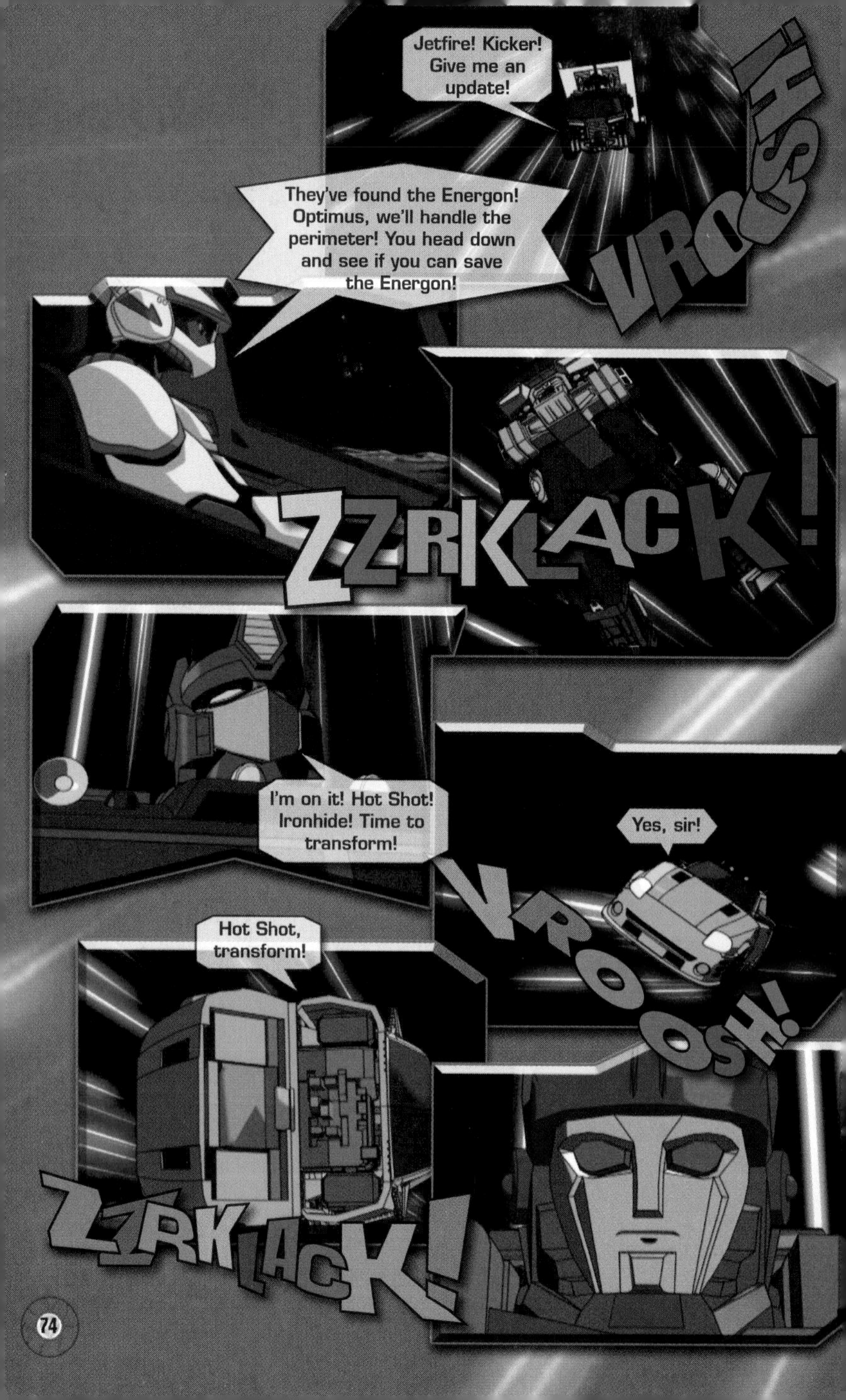

Jetfire! Kicker! Give me an update!
VROOSH!
They've found the Energon! Optimus, we'll handle the perimeter! You head down and see if you can save the Energon!
ZZRKLACK!
I'm on it! Hot Shot! Ironhide! Time to transform!
Yes, sir!
VROOOSH!
Hot Shot, transform!
ZZRKLACK!

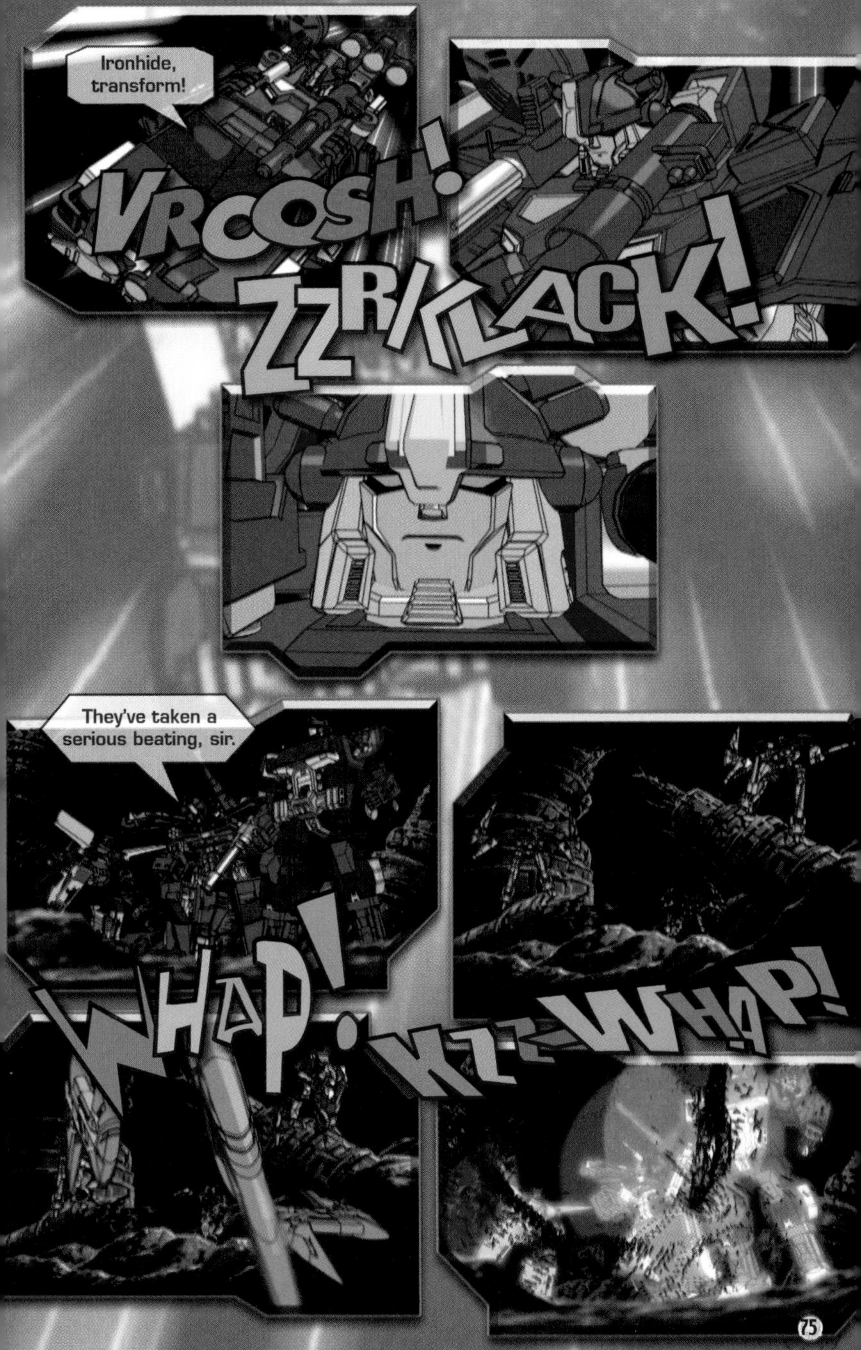
Ironhide, transform!
VRCOSH!
ZZRKLACK!
They've taken a serious beating, sir.
WHAP!
KZZ-WHAP!

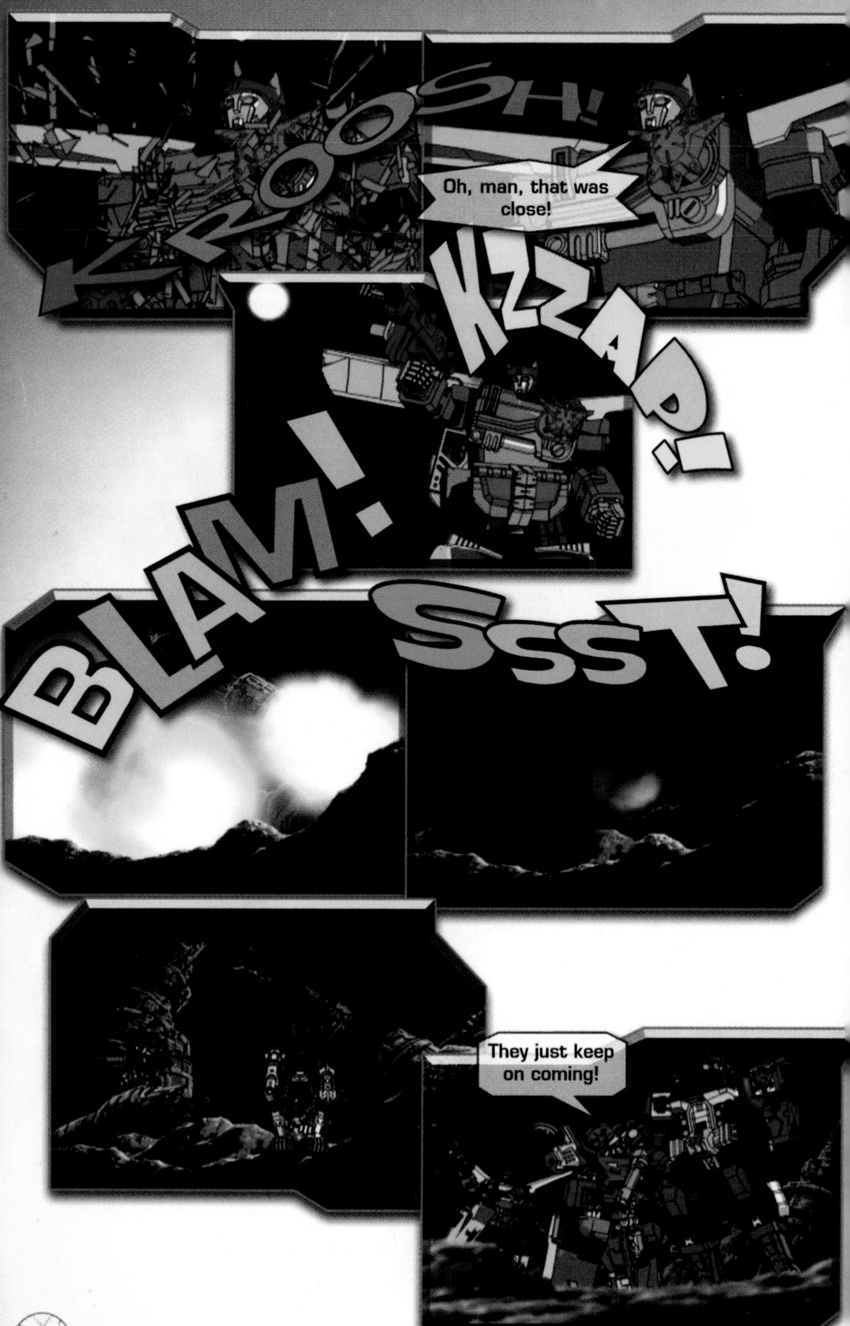
VROOOOSH!
Oh, man, that was close!
KZZAP!!
BLAM!
SSST!
They just keep on coming!

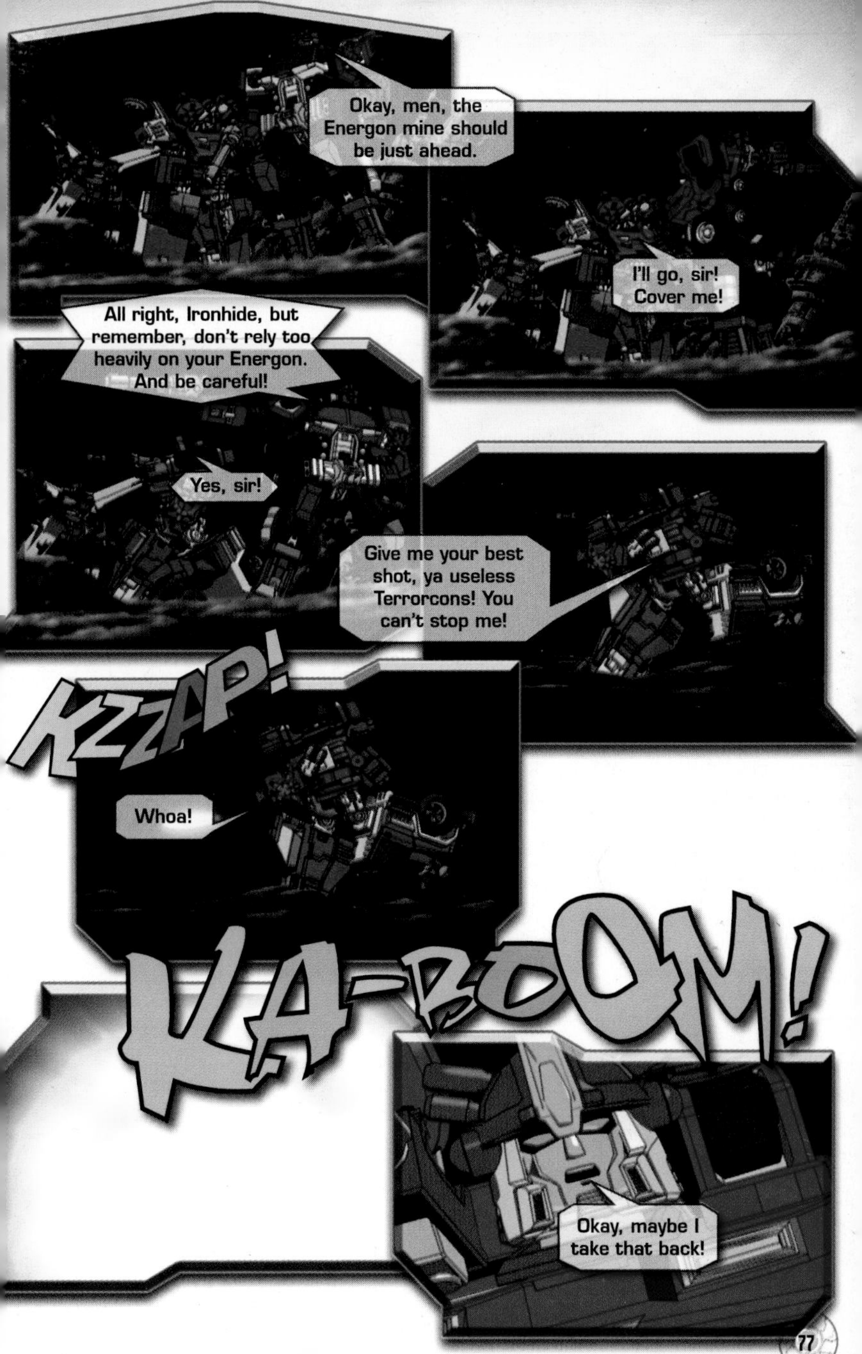
Okay, men, the Energon mine should be just ahead.
I'll go, sir! Cover me!
All right, Ironhide, but remember, don't rely too heavily on your Energon. And be careful!
Yes, sir!
Give me your best shot, ya useless Terrorcons! You can't stop me!
KZZAP!
Whoa!
KA-BOOM!
Okay, maybe I take that back!

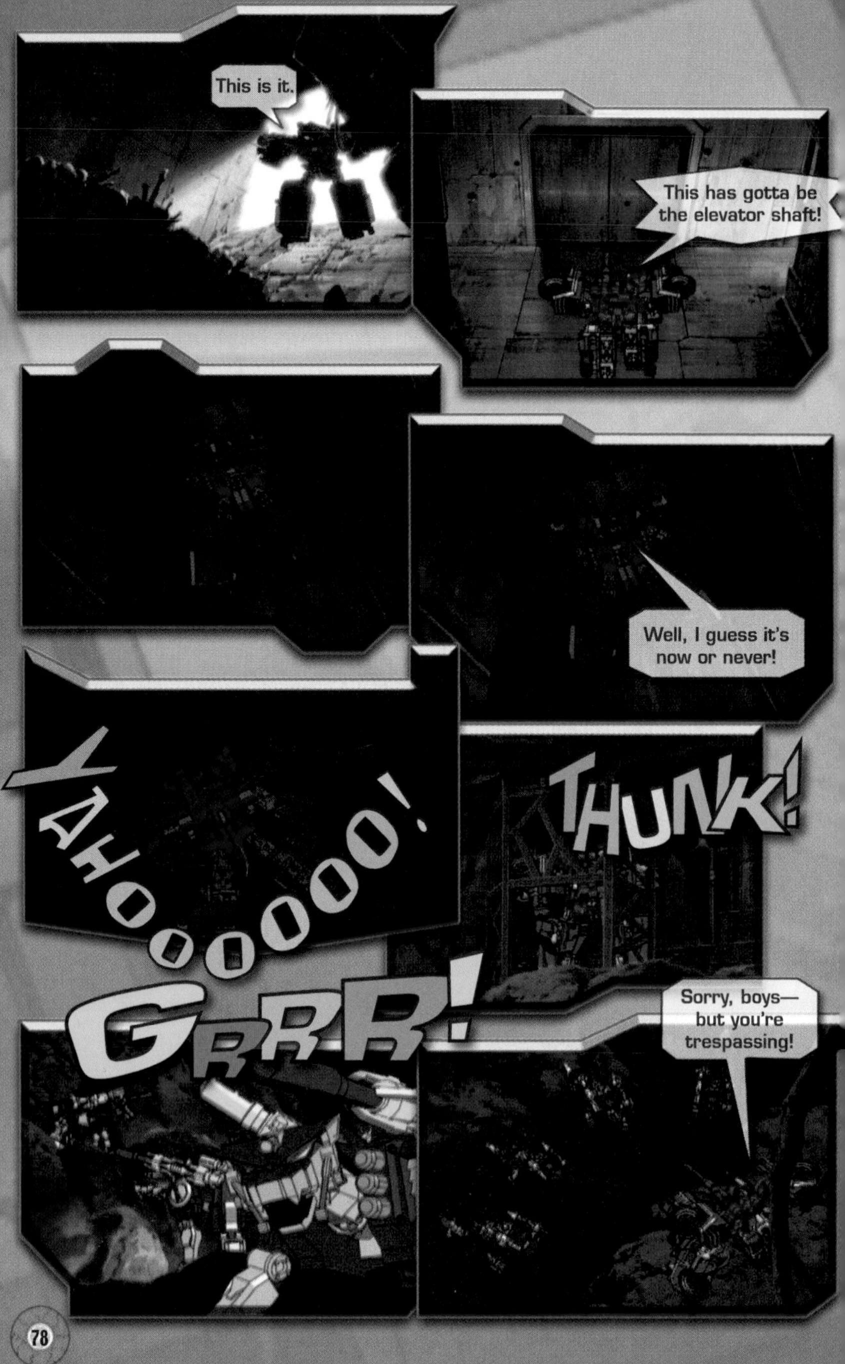

This is it.
This has gotta be the elevator shaft!
Well, I guess it's now or never!
YAHOOOOOO!
THUNK!
GRRR!
Sorry, boys—but you're trespassing!

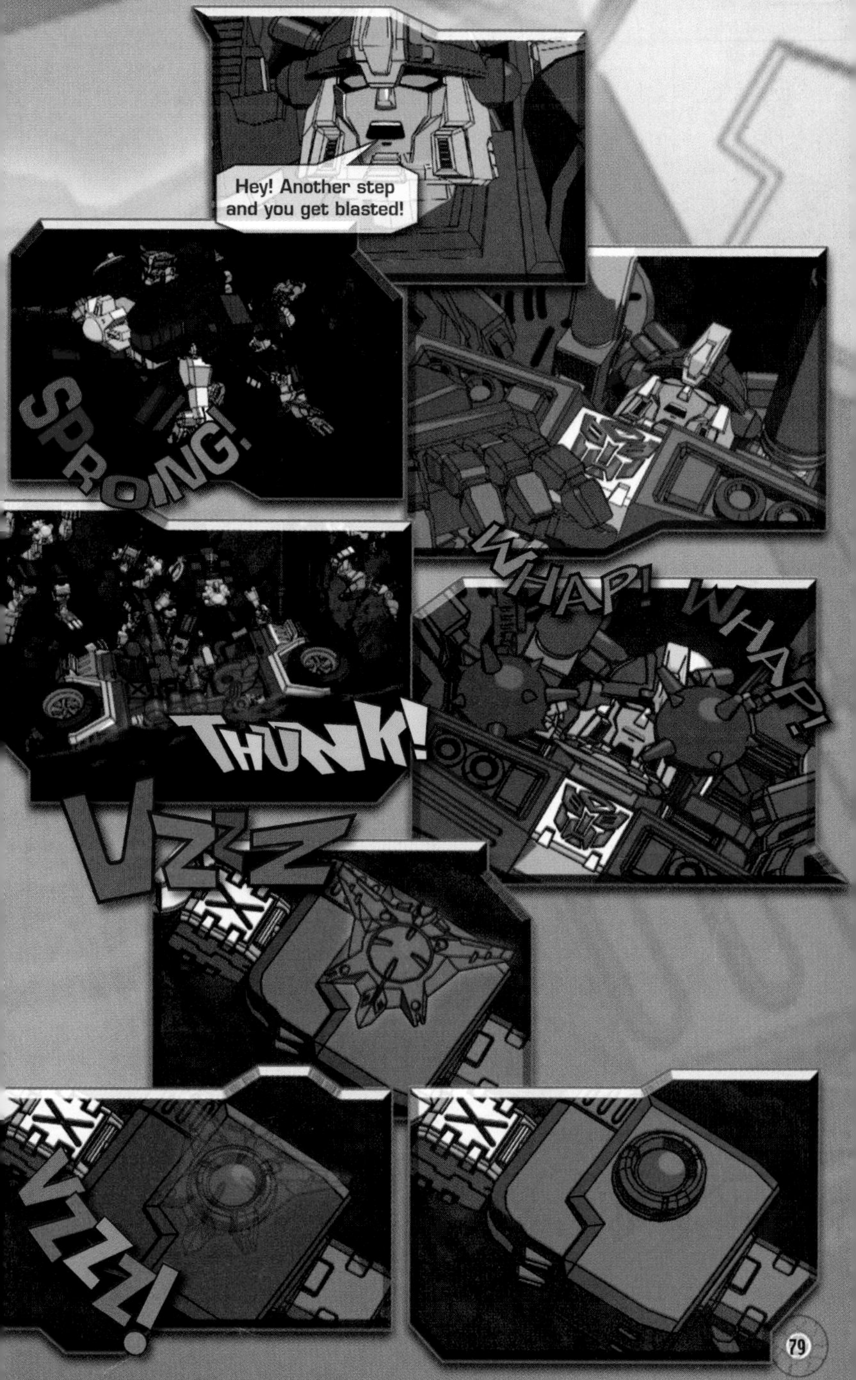

Hey! Another step and you get blasted!
SPROING!
WHAP! WHAP!
THUNK!
VZZZ
VZZZ!

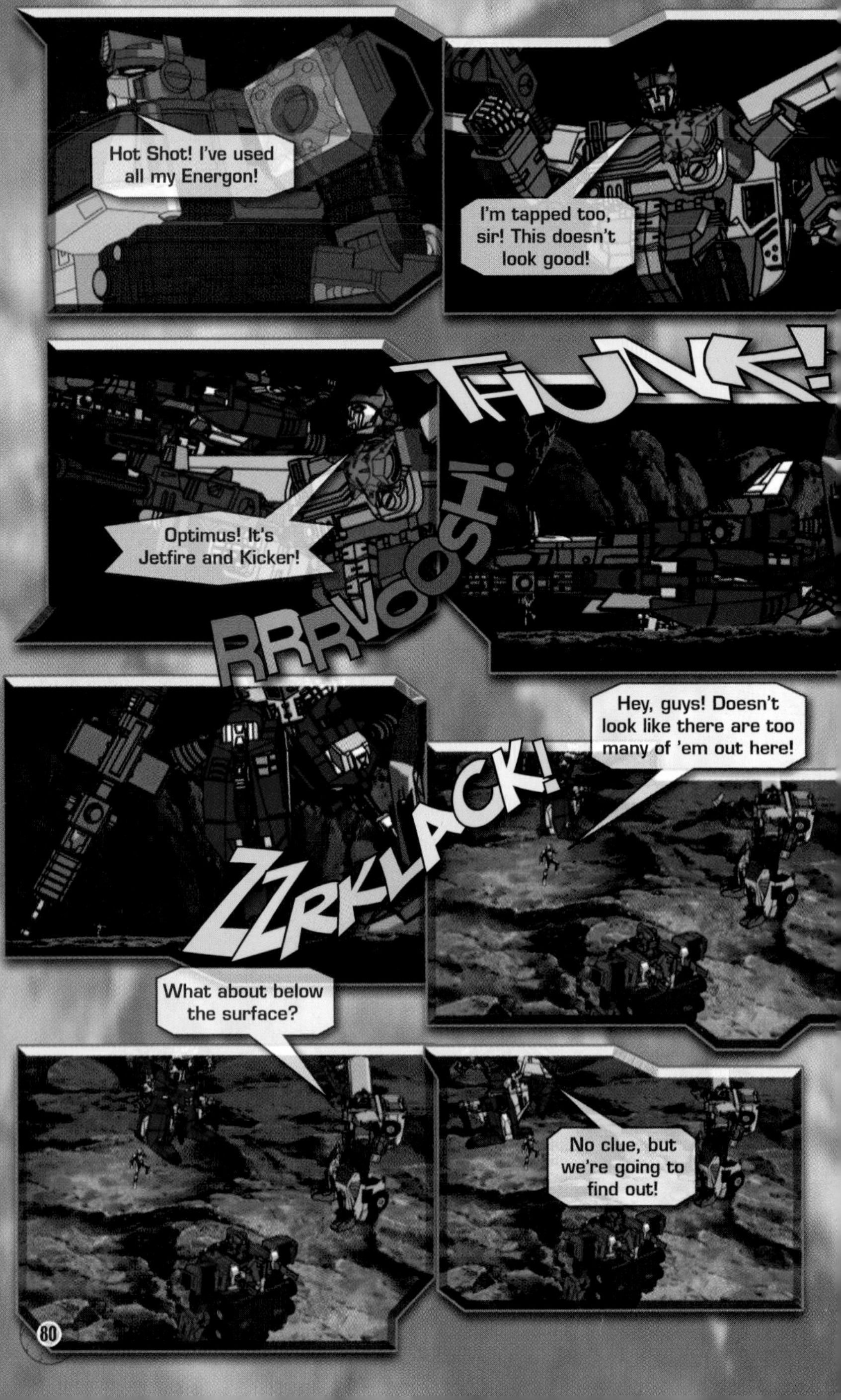

Hot Shot! I've used all my Energon!
I'm tapped too, sir! This doesn't look good!
THUNK!
Optimus! It's Jetfire and Kicker!
RRRVOOSH!
ZZRKLACK!
Hey, guys! Doesn't look like there are too many of 'em out here!
What about below the surface?
No clue, but we're going to find out!

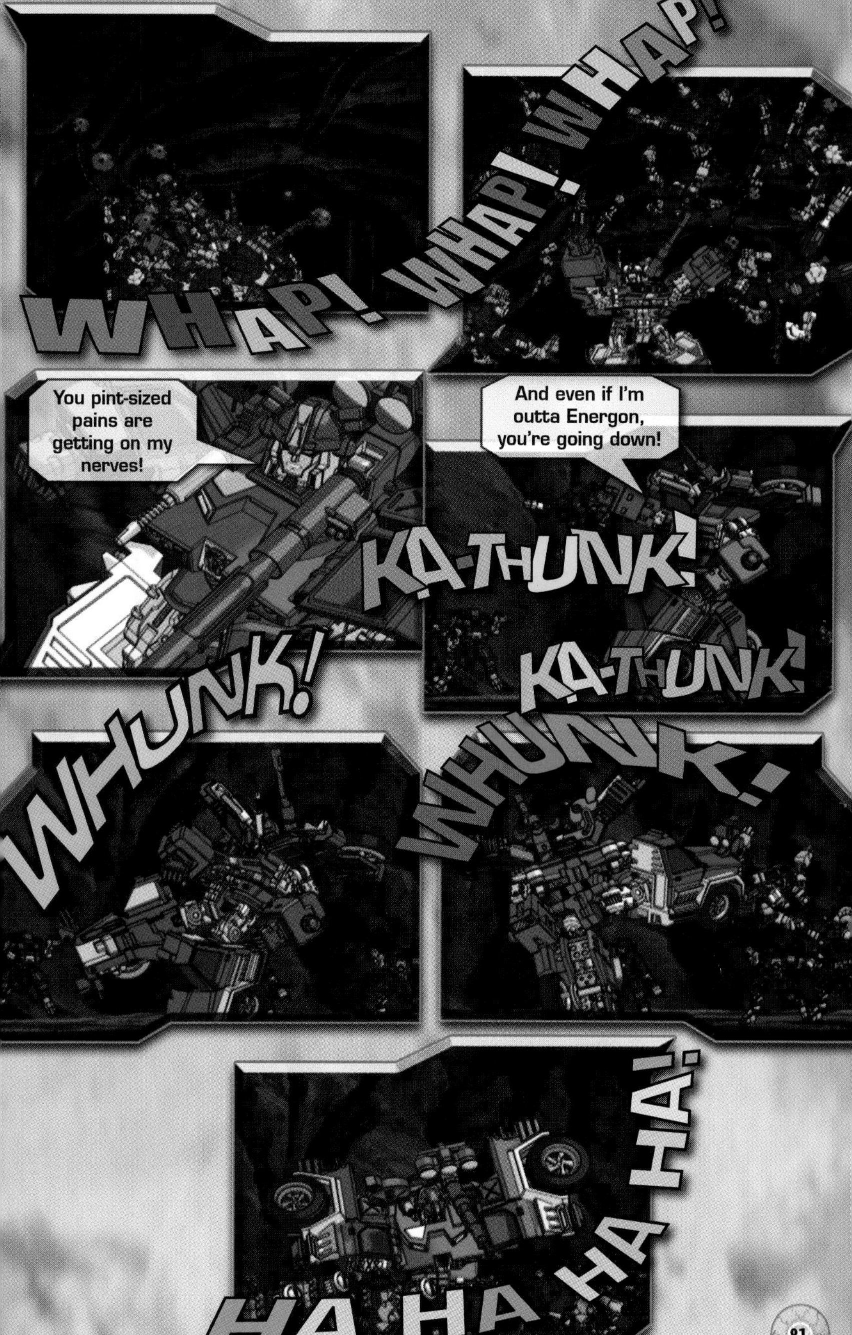
WHAP! WHAP! WHAP!
You pint-sized pains are getting on my nerves!
And even if I'm outta Energon, you're going down!
KA-THUNK!
WHUNK!
KA-THUNK!
WHUNK!
HA HA HA HA!

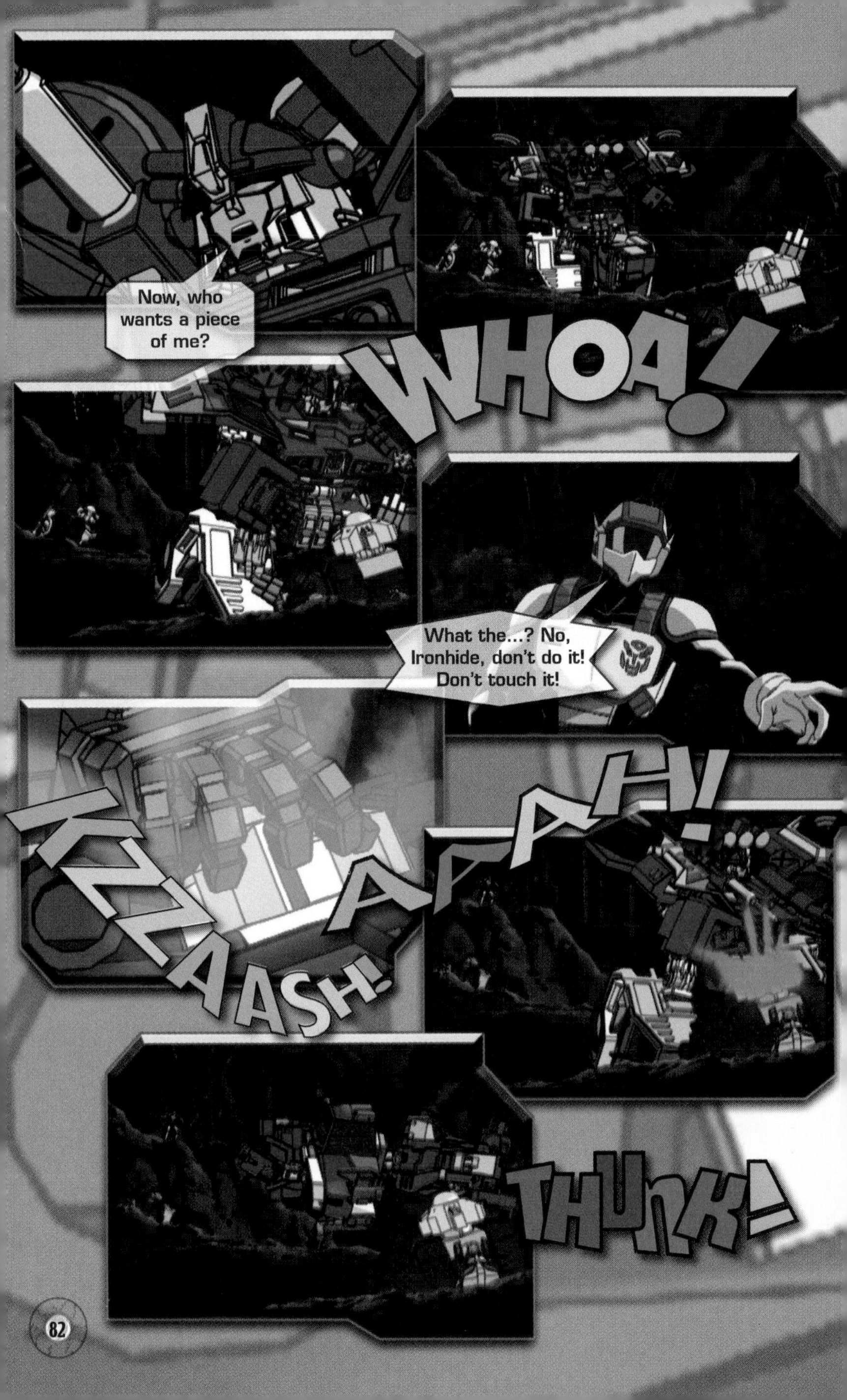
Now, who wants a piece of me?
WHOA!
What the...? No, Ironhide, don't do it! Don't touch it!
KZZAASH!
AAAAH!
THUNK!

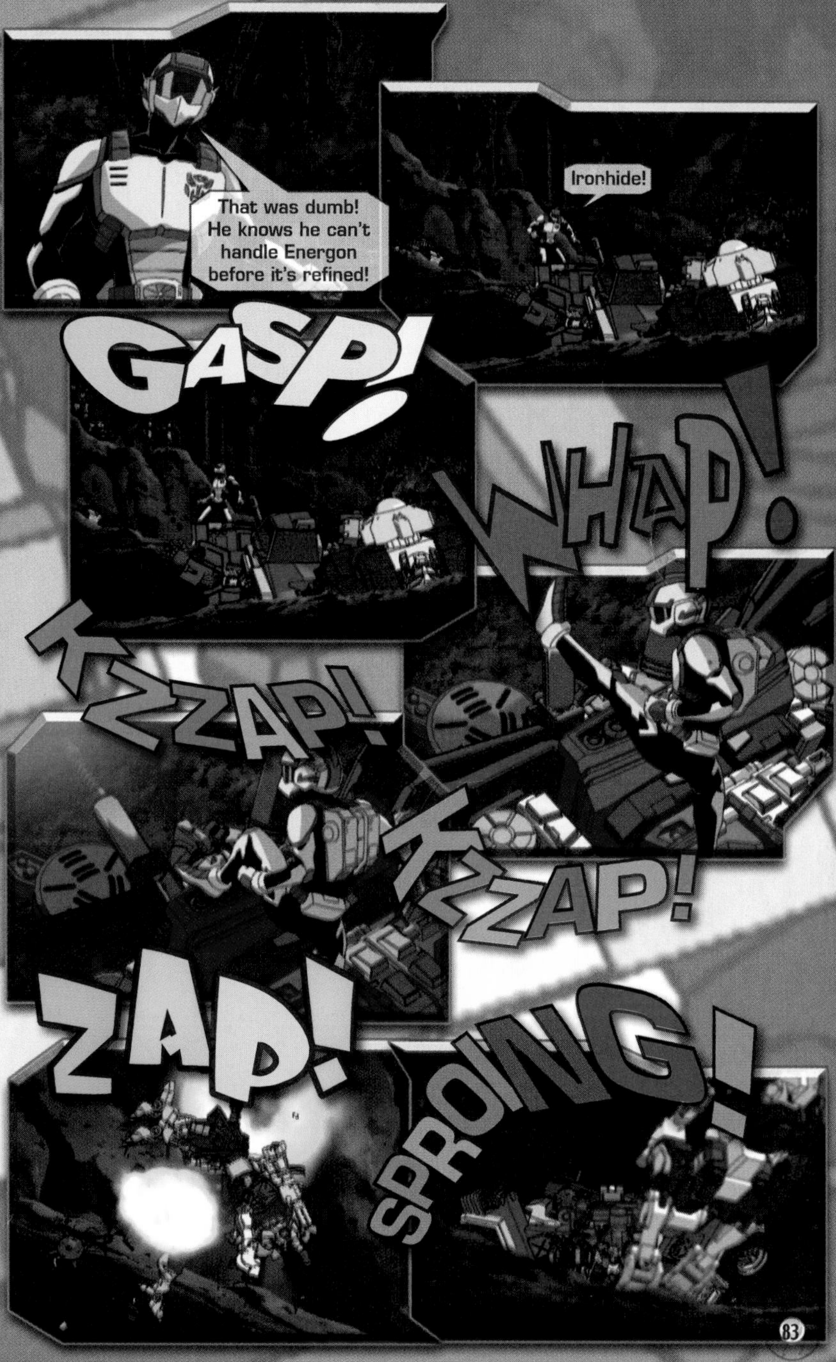
That was dumb! He knows he can't handle Energon before it's refined!
Ironhide!
GASP!
WHAP!
KZZAP!
KZZAP!
ZAP!
SPROING!

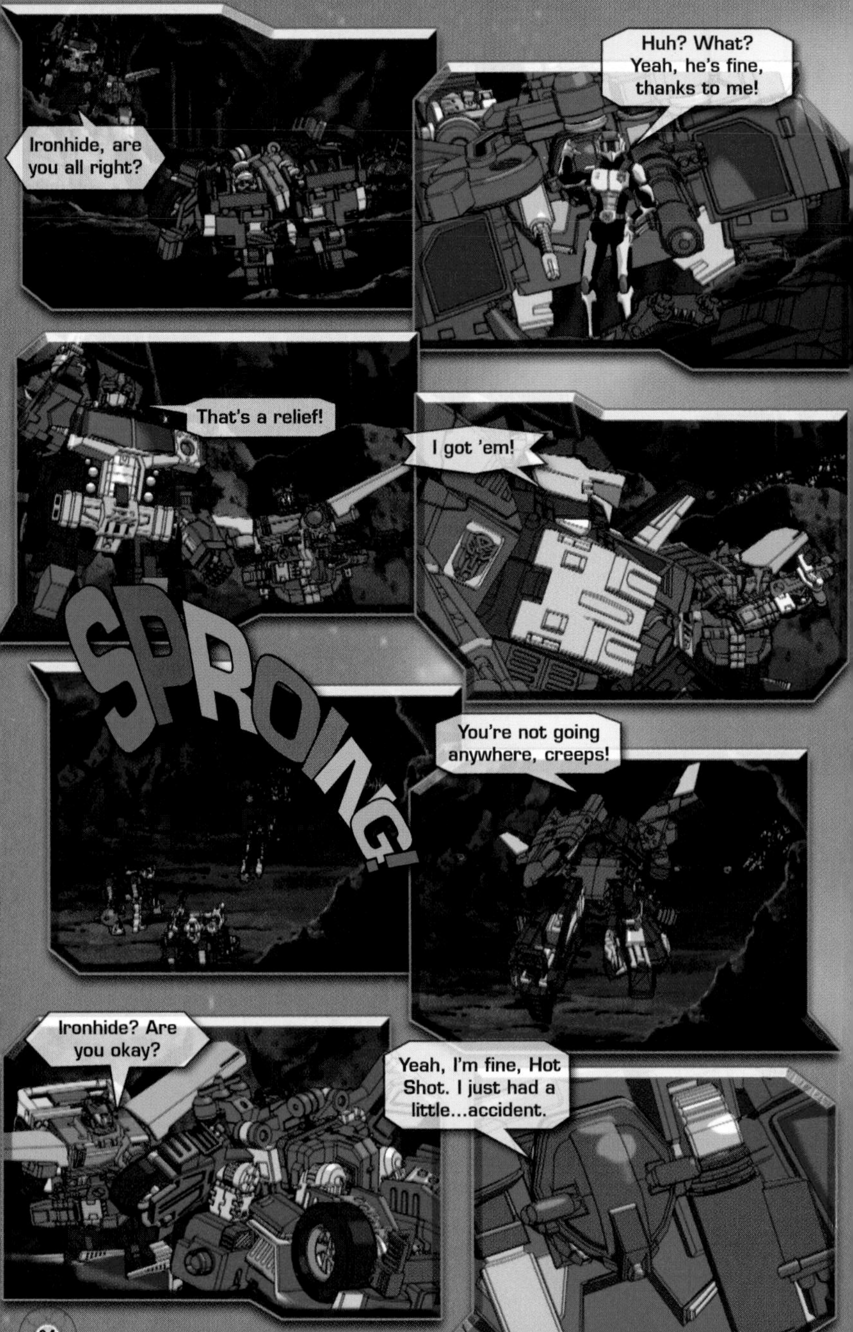
Ironhide, are you all right?
Huh? What? Yeah, he's fine, thanks to me!
That's a relief!
I got 'em!
SPROING!
You're not going anywhere, creeps!
Ironhide? Are you okay?
Yeah, I'm fine, Hot Shot. I just had a little...accident.

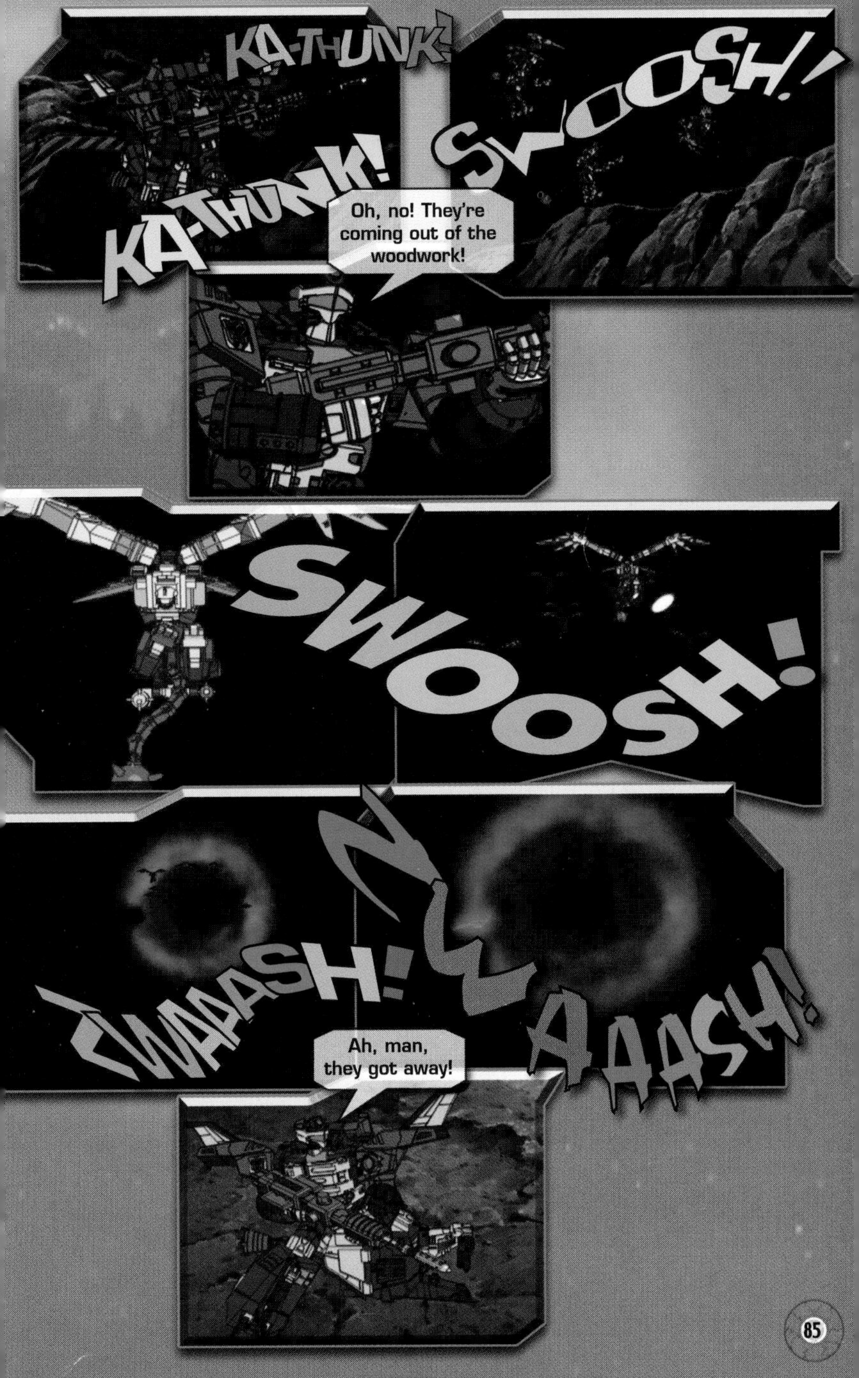
KA-THUNK!
KA-THUNK!
SWOOSH!
Oh, no! They're coming out of the woodwork!
SWOOSH!
ZWAAASH!
ZWAAASH!
Ah, man, they got away!

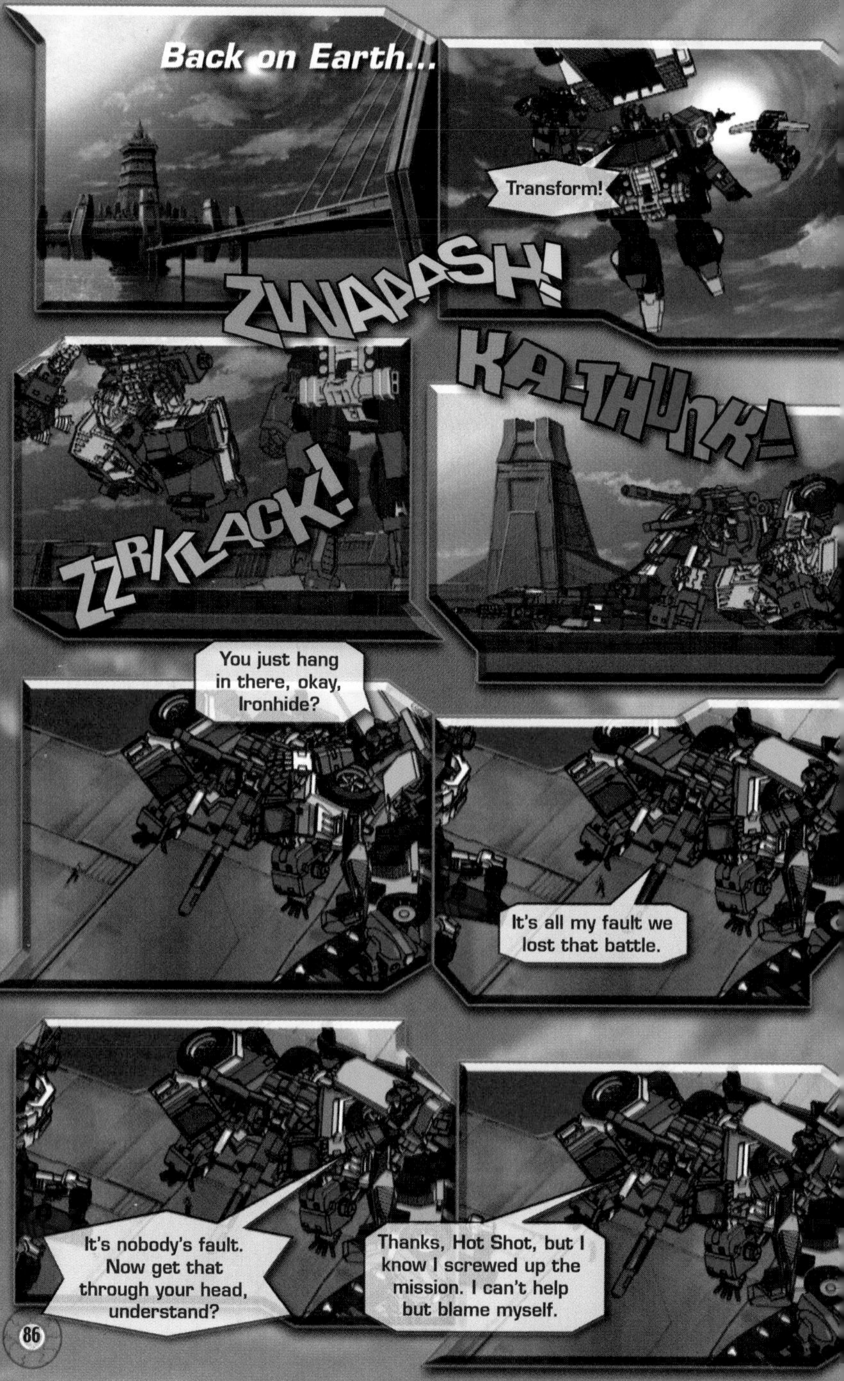
Back on Earth...
Transform!
ZWAAASH!
KA-THUNK!
ZZR/KLACK!
You just hang in there, okay, Ironhide?
It's all my fault we lost that battle.
It's nobody's fault. Now get that through your head, understand?
Thanks, Hot Shot, but I know I screwed up the mission. I can't help but blame myself.

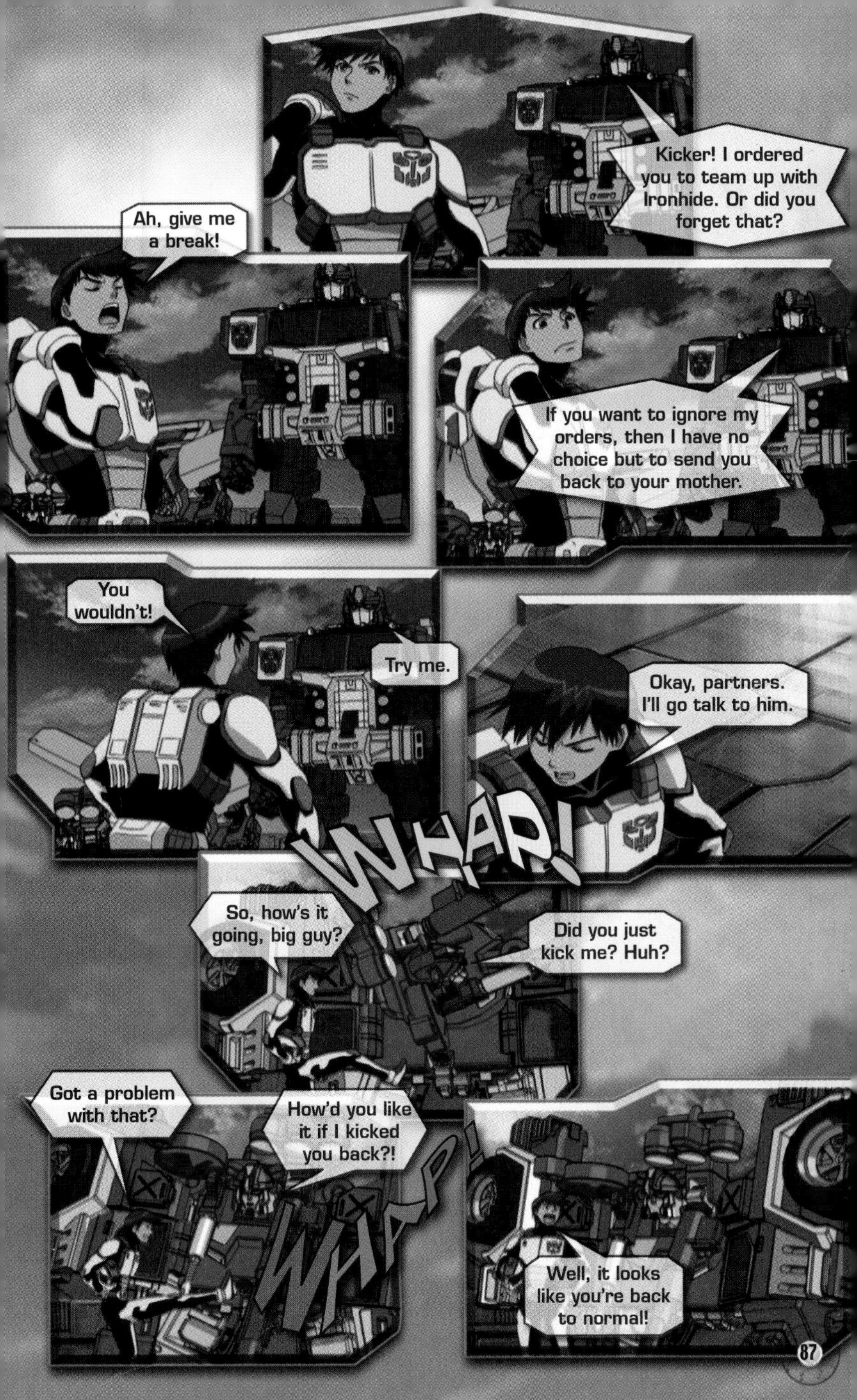
Kicker! I ordered you to team up with Ironhide. Or did you forget that?
Ah, give me a break!
If you want to ignore my orders, then I have no choice but to send you back to your mother.
You wouldn't!
Try me.
Okay, partners. I'll go talk to him.
WHAP!
So, how's it going, big guy?
Did you just kick me? Huh?
Got a problem with that?
How'd you like it if I kicked you back?!
WHAP!
Well, it looks like you're back to normal!

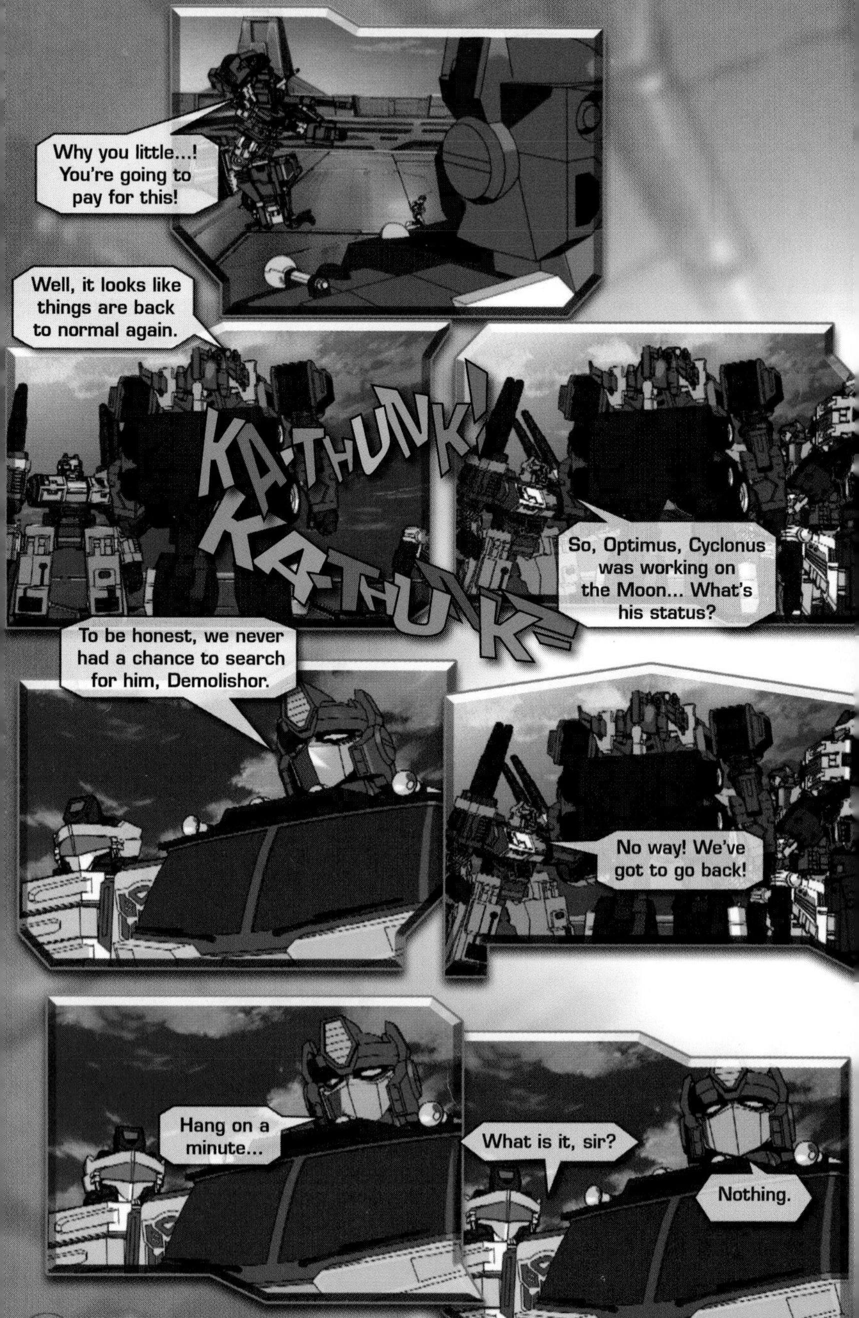
Why you little...! You're going to pay for this!
Well, it looks like things are back to normal again.
KA-THUNK!
KA-THUNK
So, Optimus, Cyclonus was working on the Moon... What's his status?
To be honest, we never had a chance to search for him, Demolishor.
No way! We've got to go back!
Hang on a minute...
What is it, sir?
Nothing.

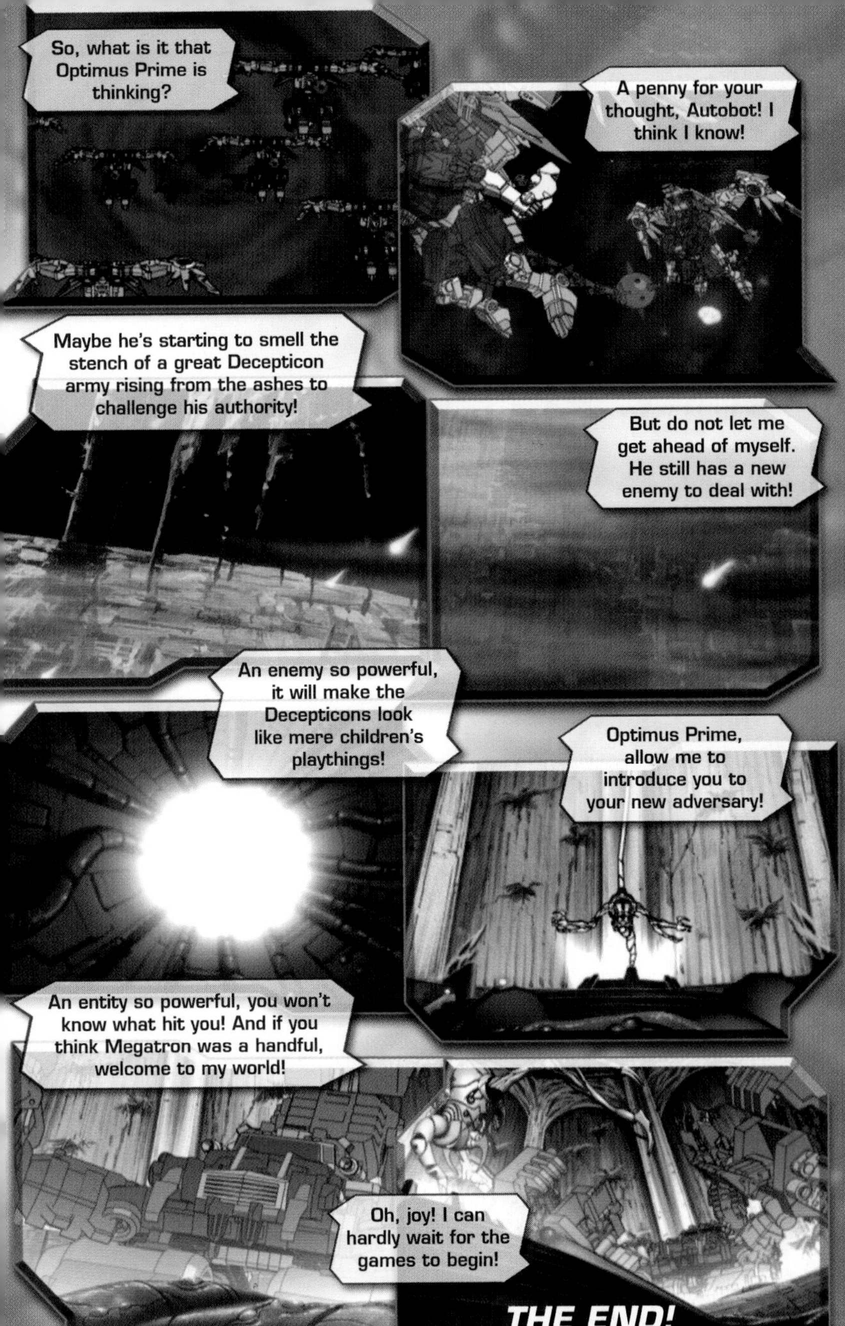
So, what is it that Optimus Prime is thinking?
A penny for your thought, Autobot! I think I know!
Maybe he's starting to smell the stench of a great Decepticon army rising from the ashes to challenge his authority!
But do not let me get ahead of myself. He still has a new enemy to deal with!
An enemy so powerful, it will make the Decepticons look like mere children's playthings!
Optimus Prime, allow me to introduce you to your new adversary!
An entity so powerful, you won't know what hit you! And if you think Megatron was a handful, welcome to my world!
Oh, joy! I can hardly wait for the games to begin!
THE END!

ALSO AVAILABLE FROM TOKYOPOP

MANGA

.HACK//LEGEND OF THE TWILIGHT
ANGELIC LAYER
BABY BIRTH
BRAIN POWERED
BRIGADOON
B'TX
CANDIDATE FOR GODDESS, THE
CARDCAPTOR SAKURA
CARDCAPTOR SAKURA - MASTER OF THE CLOW
CHRONICLES OF THE CURSED SWORD
CLAMP SCHOOL DETECTIVES
CLOVER
COMIC PARTY
CORRECTOR YUI
COWBOY BEBOP
COWBOY BEBOP: SHOOTING STAR
CRAZY LOVE STORY
CRESCENT MOON
CULDCEPT
CYBORG 009
D•N•ANGEL
DEMON DIARY
DEMON ORORON, THE
DIGIMON
DIGIMON TAMERS
DIGIMON ZERO TWO
DRAGON HUNTER
DRAGON KNIGHTS
DRAGON VOICE
DREAM SAGA
DUKLYON: CLAMP SCHOOL DEFENDERS
ET CETERA
ETERNITY
FAERIES' LANDING
FLCL
FORBIDDEN DANCE
FRUITS BASKET
G GUNDAM
GATEKEEPERS
GIRL GOT GAME
GUNDAM BLUE DESTINY
GUNDAM SEED ASTRAY
GUNDAM WING
GUNDAM WING: BATTLEFIELD OF PACIFISTS
GUNDAM WING: ENDLESS WALTZ

GUNDAM WING: THE LAST OUTPOST (G-UNIT)
HANDS OFF!
HARLEM BEAT
IMMORTAL RAIN
I.N.V.U.
INITIAL D
INSTANT TEEN: JUST ADD NUTS
JING: KING OF BANDITS
JING: KING OF BANDITS - TWILIGHT TALES
JULINE
KARE KANO
KILL ME, KISS ME
KINDAICHI CASE FILES, THE
KING OF HELL
KODOCHA: SANA'S STAGE
LEGEND OF CHUN HYANG, THE
MAGIC KNIGHT RAYEARTH I
MAGIC KNIGHT RAYEARTH II
MAN OF MANY FACES
MARMALADE BOY
MARS
MARS: HORSE WITH NO NAME
METROID
MINK
MIRACLE GIRLS
MODEL
ONE
ONE I LOVE, THE
PEACH GIRL
PEACH GIRL: CHANGE OF HEART
PITA-TEN
PLANET LADDER
PLANETES
PRINCESS AI
PSYCHIC ACADEMY
RAGNAROK
RAVE MASTER
REALITY CHECK
REBIRTH
REBOUND
RISING STARS OF MANGA
SAILOR MOON
SAINT TAIL
SAMURAI GIRL REAL BOUT HIGH SCHOOL
SEIKAI TRILOGY, THE
SGT. FROG
SHAOLIN SISTERS

03.03.04Y

ALSO AVAILABLE FROM TOKYOPOP®

For more
information visit
www.TOKYOPOP.com

03.03.04Y

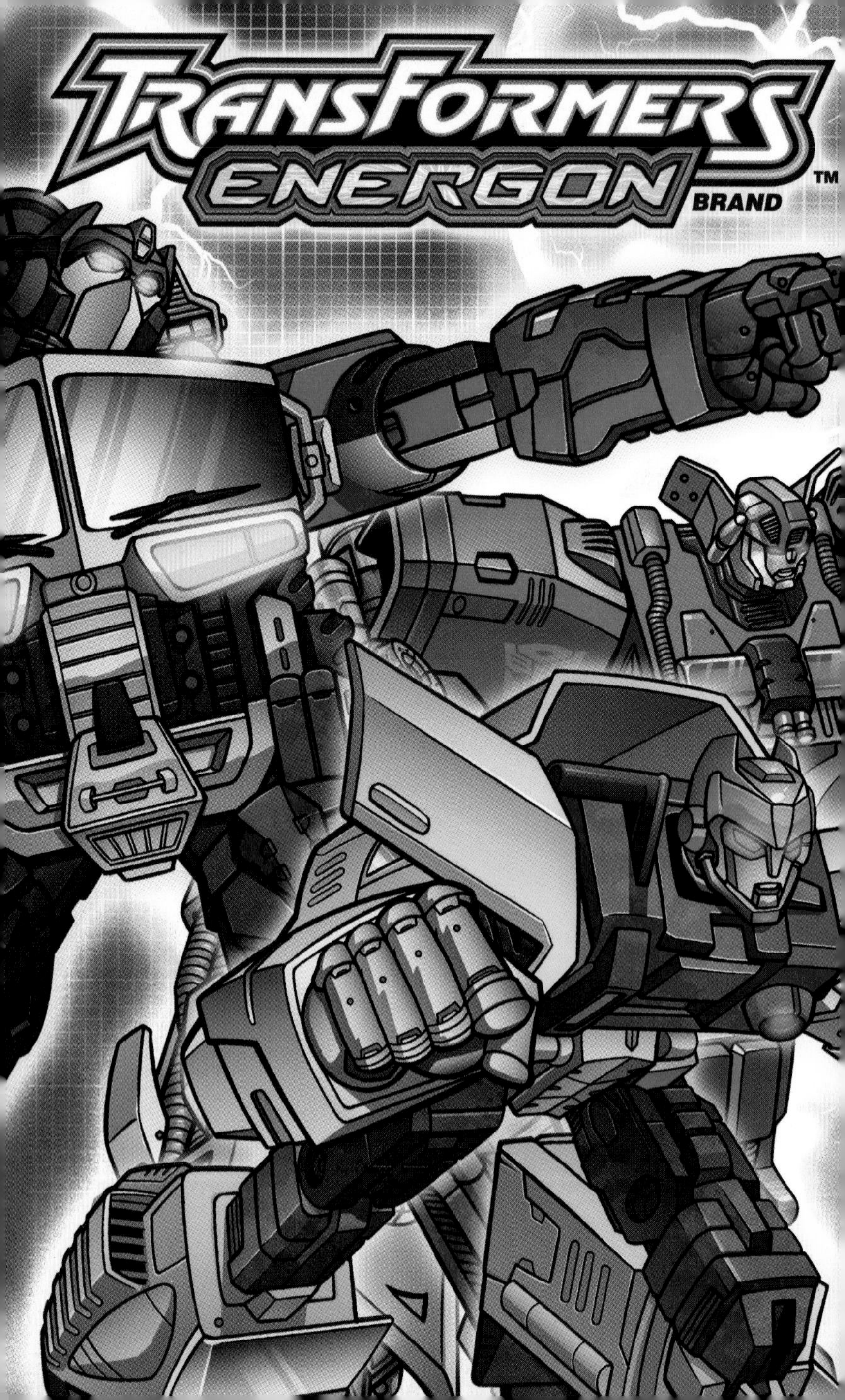
TRANSFORMERS
ENERGON
TM
BRAND

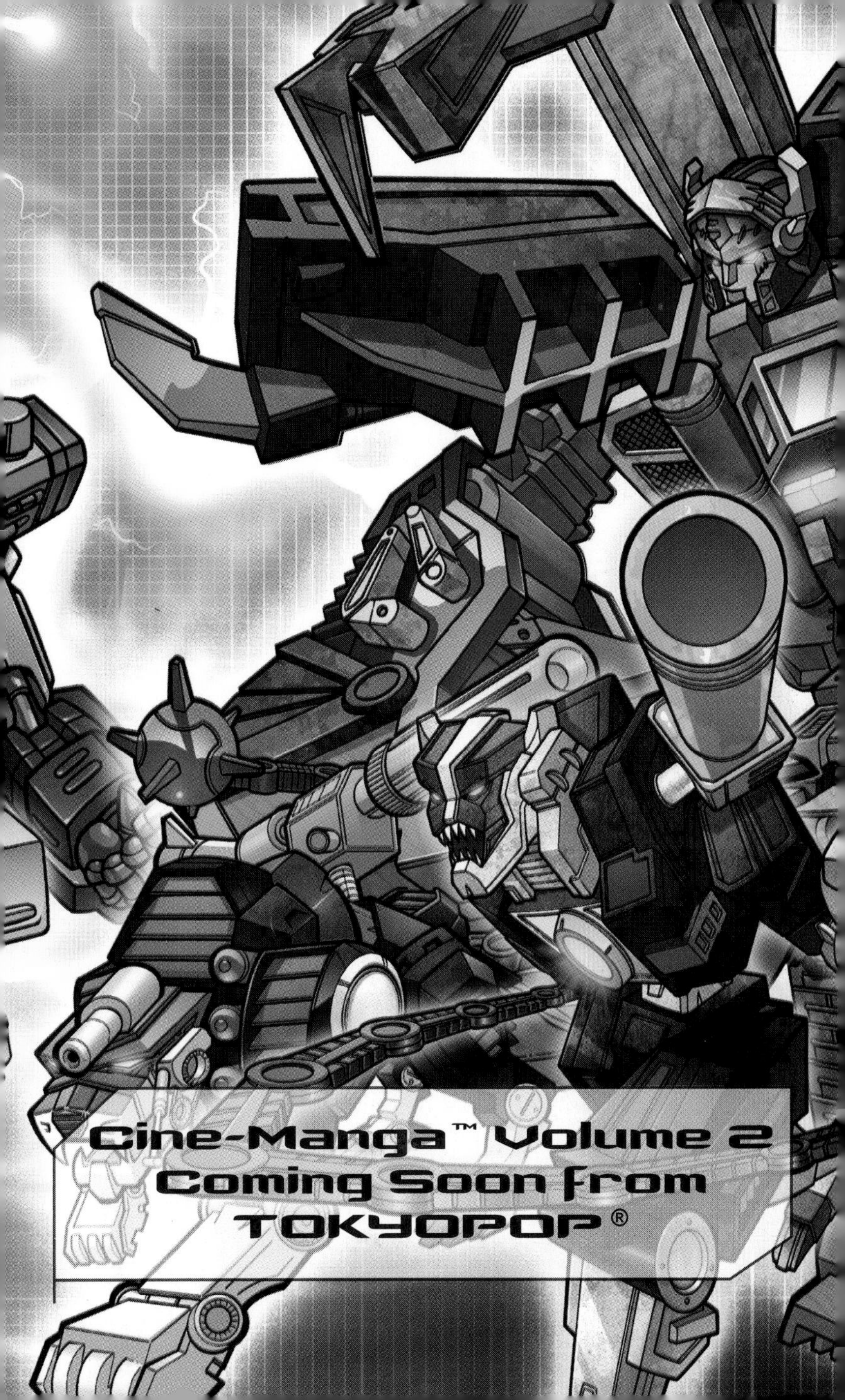
Cine-Manga™ Volume 2
Coming Soon from
TOKYOPOP®

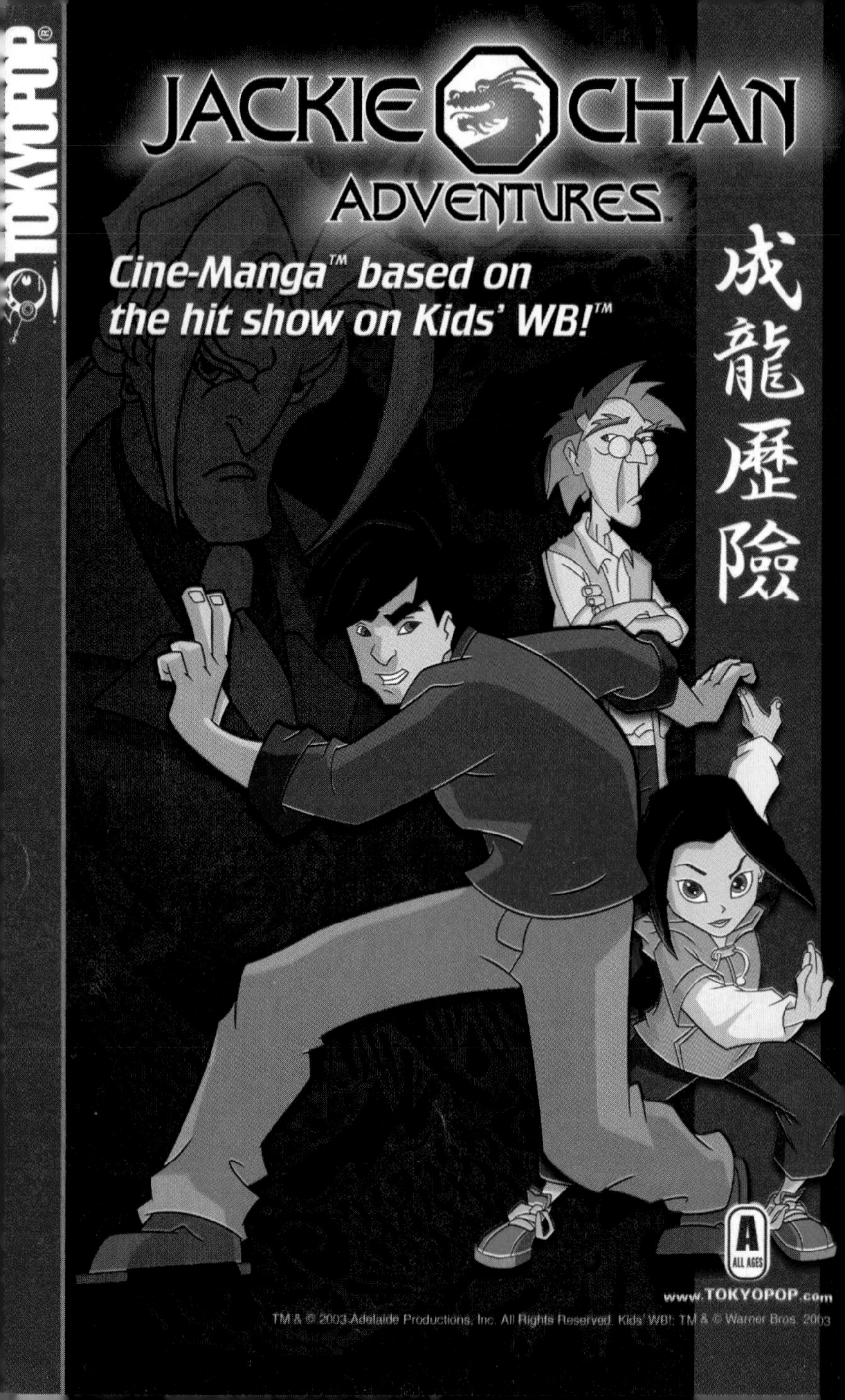
TOKYOPOP®
JACKIE CHAN
ADVENTURES™
Cine-Manga™ based on
the hit show on Kids' WB!™
成龍歷險
A ALL AGES
www.TOKYOPOP.com
TM & © 2003 Adelaide Productions, Inc. All Rights Reserved. Kids' WB!: TM & © Warner Bros. 2003

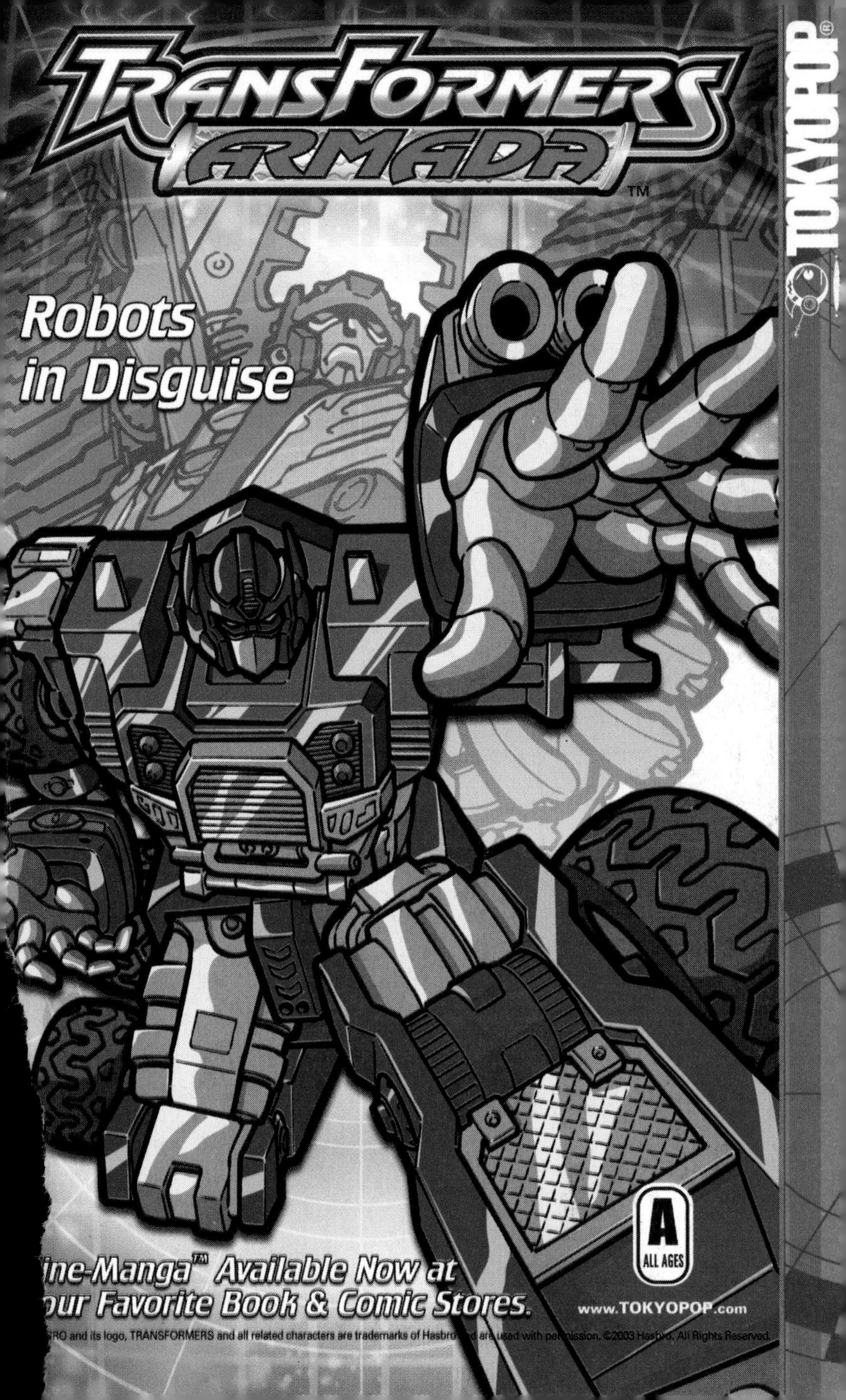
TRANSFORMERS
ARMADA
TM
TOKYOPOP
Robots
in Disguise
ALL AGES
ine-Manga™ Available Now at
our Favorite Book & Comic Stores.
www.TOKYOPOP.com
RO and its logo, TRANSFORMERS and all related characters are trademarks of Hasbro ... used with permission. ©2003 Hasbro. All Rights Reserved.

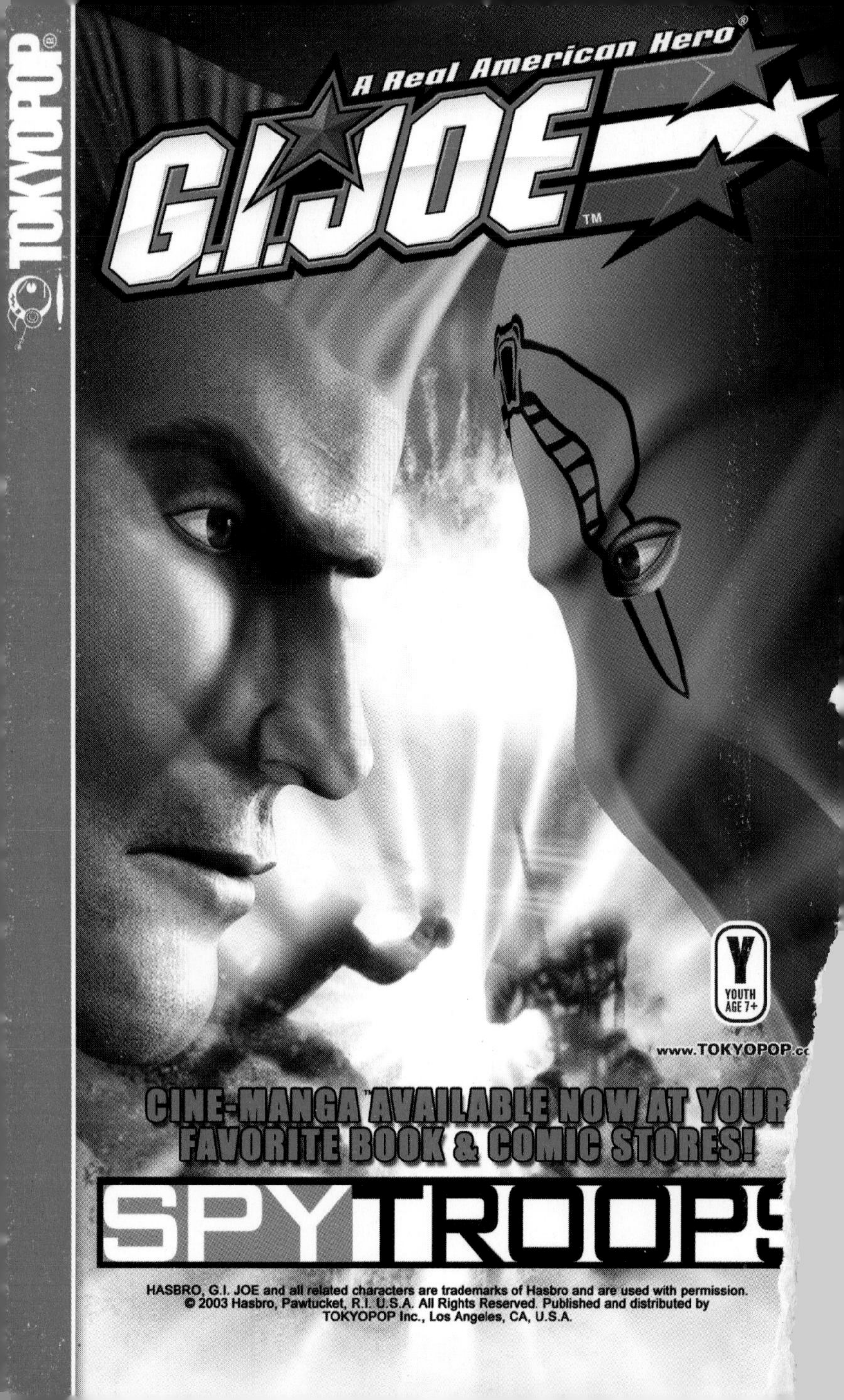
TOKYOPOP
A Real American Hero
G.I. JOE
Y
YOUTH AGE 7+
www.TOKYOPOP.co
CINE-MANGA AVAILABLE NOW AT YOUR FAVORITE BOOK & COMIC STORES!
SPY TROOP
HASBRO, G.I. JOE and all related characters are trademarks of Hasbro and are used with permission.
© 2003 Hasbro, Pawtucket, R.I. U.S.A. All Rights Reserved. Published and distributed by TOKYOPOP Inc., Los Angeles, CA, U.S.A.